# THE LAST GREAT LEAP

The age of participatory evolution has begun.
In BRAVE NEW BABY, discover:

- A self-designed human who has realized
  his oldest, fondest wish—immortality
- Baby markets where prospective parents
  can shop for a frozen embryo
- The astronaut perfectly bred for alien environments: a creature with four legs—or
  none
- Viruses as a tool for genetic surgery
- A man who can prowl jungles with a leopard's instincts or swim oceans with a dolphin's cunning
- Marvelous machines that let us dial our
  dreams

Does it sound incredible? Perhaps it does. Yet
many of these innovations are as close as tomorrow—in an ever-accelerating revolution
toward a future beyond our wildest imaginings.

**Books by David M. Rorvik**

As Man Becomes Machine
Brave New Baby
In His Image

Published by POCKET BOOKS

# BRAVE NEW BABY

## PROMISE AND PERIL OF THE BIOLOGICAL REVOLUTION

# DAVID RORVIK

PUBLISHED BY POCKET BOOKS NEW YORK

## PERMISSIONS

"Into the World of Brave New Baby" is based on "And Now: The
Evolution Revolution," published in *Avant-Garde* magazine. Reprinted
by permission of *Avant-Garde* magazine. Copyright © 1970 by Avant-
Garde Media, Inc.

"New Hope for the Infertile" is based on "Hope and Help for the Infertile," published in *Good Housekeeping*. Used by permission of the
Hearst Corporation. Copyright © 1970 by Hearst Corporation.

I would like to thank all the doctors, scientists, engineers and technicians who gave so generously of their time and patience in providing the data and explaining the procedures discussed in this book. And special thanks to Gail Lowman for invaluable technical assistance.

# FOR
# SENLIN

# Contents

# BRAVE NEW BABY

# INTRODUCTION

Into the World
of Brave New Baby

*Under the magic wand of biology, man is now gradually becoming quite different from what he was. Here and now he is changing into a new and paradoxical animal, unknown to those who assign names to things, an animal with a special pied physiology. Here and now Homo sapiens is in the process of becoming Homo biologicus—a strange biped that will combine the properties of self-reproduction without males, like the green fly; of fertilizing his female at long distance, like the nautiloid mollusks; of changing sex, like the xiphophores; of growing from cuttings, like the earthworm; of replacing his missing parts, like the newt; of developing outside his mother's body, like the kangaroo; and of hibernating, like the hedgehog.*

With this rhapsodic passage, translated here from *Peut-On Modifier l'Homme? (Can Man Be Modified?)*, famed biologist Jean Rostand penned what may come to be remembered as the preamble to the Biological Revolution—a revolution that has burst upon us with an impact that is bound to be felt for centuries to come. In history books yet unwritten, the remarkable discoveries of the mid-twentieth century will be underscored to mark the beginning of a new epoch easily as significant as the one in which man evolved from ape. This is the new era of "Participatory Evolution." No longer is man the offspring of Nature, the creature of natural selection. Science has provided him with the technology to become his *own* maker.

Dr. Edward L. Tatum, Nobel Prize man, calls man's growing ability to engineer his own genetic future, "the most astounding prospect so far suggested by science." And Caltech biologist Robert L. Sinsheimer terms it "one of the most important concepts to arise in the history of mankind," adding that "for the first time in all time, a living creature understands its origins and can undertake to design its future."

But while science soars ahead in the light of this brilliant new dawn, some fear that society as a whole will continue to sleep, dreaming what has gone before, not what is to come. Society and its laws have, undeniably, lagged painfully far behind science during the industrial and technological revolutions. Society now stands in peril of becoming hopelessly lost in the wake of the Biological Revolution—*unless,* as Dr. Jonas Salk puts it, "the managers of society are given some advance notice of what may be in store." What follows, then, is not only a description of man's new creative prowess, but also an attempt to define some of the problems society will have to resolve if it is not to give way entirely to a technocratic elite.

If this particular revolution—and the "brave new baby" that it will produce—had any one father, it would probably have to be the late Dr. Hermann J. Muller, winner of the Nobel Prize in physiology and medicine. This scientific visionary repeatedly startled the world with a program for genetic betterment called "Germinal Choice." His plan called on parents to forgo egotistical desires to reproduce their own genetic characteristics, to utilize sex *only* for pleasure, not for propagation. To populate the earth, and at the same time improve the basic model of man (the so-called "human genotype"), Dr. Muller proposed a program of artificial insemination, using the sperm of a select group of men, chosen for physical

fitness and mental acuity. Women deemed fit to have
children would be permitted, perhaps with assistance
from their husbands, to pick sperm donors from this
pool of men. In sharp contrast with the current pol-
icy of strict donor anonymity, Dr. Muller called for
detailed dossiers on all donors to help the prospective parents make a wise choice.

Critics of the plan said it was imbued "with the odor
of the human stud farm." And lack of donor anonymity, they charged, would greatly accentuate the legal
and emotional problems of artificial insemination.
In cases where the donor is known, they asked, could
he be sued for child support should the mother's husband divorce or abandon her? Could the donor be
named as a correspondent in a divorce proceeding?
Could the administering doctor or the donor be
charged with adultery? Could the wife similarly be
charged? Could the AI offspring claim to be heirs of
the donor in an estate settlement? And so on. These
are not fanciful questions; there are lawsuits revolving
around them in the courts today. Not long ago,
for example, a woman was given custody of a child
conceived by artificial insemination. An Oklahoma
court turned down her husband's request for visiting
privileges on the grounds that he was not the child's
biological father. The fact that he was the only father
the child had ever known apparently counted for nothing.

To skirt these problems, Dr. Muller urged widespread establishment of frozen sperm banks. These
banks would administer only those sperm specimens
that had been in storage for at least twenty years or
obtained from donors who had since died. Though Dr.
Muller's dynamic program—backed in part by such
scientific luminaries as Sir Julian Huxley and Nobelist
F. H. C. Crick—has yet to be implemented, artificial
insemination is rapidly coming into its own, account-
ing for some ten thousand births each year. And
frozen-sperm banks—some of which may be used to
keep a sperm supply viable even in the event of nu-

clear war—are springing up all over. Dr. Jerome G. Sherman, a pioneer in this field, estimates that there are already hundreds of healthy babies conceived from sperm frozen for long periods of time.

Now egg- and embryo-implantation techniques promise to make possible a *complete* program of germinal choice. As you will see, later in this book, scientists have already succeeded in removing fertilized egg cells from prize cows and implanting them in genetically less desirable animals, which carry the embryos through to birth as if they were their own. Fertilization is achieved through artificial insemination, using only the sperm of choice bulls. The prize cows, freed from the burdens of pregnancy, can go on supplying egg cells to be implanted in other animals. In this way a prize herd can rapidly be built up. A cow that might have had only eight or nine calves in its lifetime instead mothers hundreds.

Now scientists are poised and ready to apply this remarkable technique to man—not ten or twenty years from now, as was predicted by some skeptics only a few years ago, but *right now*. And it is a technique that will be used not only to improve the quality of man, but to give the barren woman the fulfilling experience of childbirth, and the wealthy woman the opportunity to avoid the rigors of pregnancy and still have children of her own.

Hence, as Jean Rostand has noted, man is on the verge of an era in which reproduction no longer demands the actual physical union of two human beings. The genetic characteristics of a man and a woman can now be combined across vast distances of space *and* time. Man, Rostand has observed, will have to adjust to the notion before very long that children can be born of parents who have been long dead or separated by continents their entire lives.

Though artificial insemination and the techniques of egg and embryo implantation have mind-stretching implications for society, man will be called on to make even bigger adjustments in his thinking when science usurps man's most sacred institution—motherhood—and makes it the prerogative of the test tube rather than of the womb. Already science has learned how to husband the miracle of conception *outside* the human body, successfully joining sperm and egg cells together in a test tube to form new life. Still other scientists have been busy these past several years creating artificial placentas and wombs—the instruments necessary to sustain these brave new babies of the test tube and carry them through to "birth" in a world of plastic and stainless steel, rather than of flesh and blood.

At the same time, a new breed of medical specialists called fetologists are exploring the world of "the littlest astronaut," the fetus. This sphere, previously considered sacrosanct, is now being probed with bold new techniques designed to detect genetic defects in time to do something about them. On the frontier of this new science is fetal surgery: the actual removal, treatment and reimplantation of the developing fetus. All of this is expected to stand science in good stead when "ectogenesis," or complete test-tube pregnancy, becomes a reality. By then, Rostand noted, "it will be little more than a game to change the subject's sex, the color of its eyes, the general proportions of body and limbs, and perhaps the facial features." Similarly, as science gains increased access to the developing fetus, the possibility of programing personality and increasing intelligence will be considerably enhanced.

As for changing, controlling and selecting sex, the research is already yielding significant results. Lab animals treated with hormones have undergone complete sexual transformations. Embryos originally destined to be males turn out at birth to be females, capable of reproduction, and vice versa. Another doctor has worked out a set of easy procedures by which prospective parents can attempt—with an 80 per cent chance of success—to select the sex of their children.

Dramatic—and sometimes frightening—as these advances are, the doors to an even more astounding future have been flung open by discovery of the structure of DNA, the essence of biological inner space and the chemical code of life. Now that man has broken that code, he can undertake to manipulate the DNA molecules and the genes that make it up, thus becoming master of his own heredity. "Genetic surgery" is the term Dr. Tatum and others have coined to describe manipulation of DNA. Dr. Tatum foresees the day when geneticists will be able to delete undesirable genes, insert others and mechanically or chemically transform still others—foreordaining, at the molecular level, the physical, mental and even racial characteristics of the incipient individual. All of this, Dr. Joshua Lederberg, another Nobel Prize-winning geneticist, believes could become a reality within one or two decades, provided an aggressive program of research is sustained.

But perhaps even before man is deleting unwanted genes with "laser erasers" and inserting others with "viral transducers," he will be manipulating the chromosomal content of DNA in such a way that sex will no longer play any part in reproduction. Indeed, a means of asexual propagation has already been achieved with certain plants and animals. "Cloning," as it is called, not only results in offspring that have only one parent (*either* male or female) but also in offspring that are exact *replicas* of that single parent. And such eminent scientists as Dr. Lederberg believe that this procedure will soon be applied to man, for good or bad, possibly resulting in tribes or armies of identical twins! This procedure, along with some of the problems it may produce, is discussed at length in a later chapter.

Man will never be entirely satisfied with running off carbon copies of existing human models; he will inevitably set out to make new ones. Human hybrids are just around the corner; before long, some scientists hope—and others fear—man will be bred for specific jobs and specific environments, for life under the sea as well as life on distant planets. Molecular manipulation promises to provide us not only with new appendages and greater physical versatility but also with sweeping mastery over the mind and possibly even with immortality. "Memory editing" and "education by injection" are just two of the revolutionary possibilities seriously contemplated by many scientists today.

Beyond genetic manipulation, there lies another facet of Participatory Evolution, one even more breathtaking than test-tube birth, clonal propagation and hybridization. It can be summed up in one word: "cyborg." The cyborg—or cybernetic organism—is part man, part machine. It defines a new rung on the evolutionary ladder and points to what may be man's ultimate destiny. Already there are cyborgs among us—individuals with dacron arteries, ceramic hip joints, silicone breasts, pacemakers, electronic bladders, plastic corneas and so on. Eventually, many scientists are convinced, man will become almost indistinguishable from machine, having discarded all his bodily parts (except, possibly, his brain) for more durable, if not immortal, mechanical components.

Cybernetic experts are talking seriously about brain-computer symbiotes—systems in which brains and computers are intimately linked—right now, and some foresee the day when man will discard even his brain, having first programed all of its knowledge and personality into the computer part of his being.

There *may* exist an evolutionary rung one step beyond even the cyborg. The astrophysicist and writer Arthur C. Clarke believes that man—or cyborg, as he will then be—will eventually grow weary of corporeal existence in any form. The final evolutionary step will come, then, when he learns how to translate his being into "frozen lattices of light," becoming a creature of electromagnetic radiation, able to probe the far reaches of the universe with the speed and agility of light, "free at last," in Clarke's words "from the tyranny of matter."

# I.

---

# BRAVE NEW
# BABY *NOW*

The Biological Revolution, which sees man taking dominion over himself, becoming, for better or worse, his own maker, is no longer the stuff of science fiction and wide-eyed fantasy. It is happening—here and now. Life is being shaped, controlled and even *created* by man in ways that would have been impossible, not to mention heretical, only a few years ago. For centuries, man has had to adhere to dictums asserting his own impotence, to the notion, for example, that children are gifts of God and that their absence is an expression of His wrath, that the fetus in the womb is an untouchable, a mysterious creature that must not be tampered with or ministered to in any way, that the sex of one's children is determined by the whims of God or nature and can never be wholly controlled by man, that one must be grateful for what one gets (even if it's a girl again—for the fourth time), that a woman, in order to be a mother, must endure the long rigors of pregnancy.

Now these dicta—along with man's impotence—are crumbling. In Chapter One of this section ("New Hope for the Infertile"), you will discover that, thanks to medical science, new life is emerging where previously there was only that implacable wall called "God's will." While Chapter One will be of special interest to those who number among the twelve million who suffer from infertility in this country, Chapter Two ("Embryo Implants: A Startling New Way to Have a Baby") will be of general interest. It outlines some very nearly foolproof methods of overcoming infertility but goes far beyond this to show how it is possible, for example, for a woman to have children that are biologically her own, *without* going through pregnancy.

Chapter Three ("Selecting the Sex of Your Baby") deals with the safe, easy-to-follow procedures devised by a leading gynecologist and designed to help prospective parents *choose* the sex of their children, rather than settle for whatever Mother Nature decides to give them. And in the final chapter of this opening section ("Fetal Surgery: Operating on the Unborn") we enter the previously forbidden world of the womb on an awesome mission to save life *before* birth.

# ONE

# New Hope
# for the Infertile

"For five years it went on," Mrs. D. said, obviously pained by the memory. "I saw one doctor after another in three different states. I would sit in their offices surrounded by women who were gloriously pregnant and feel like an outcast. These other women would look at me, as if to say, 'What are *you* doing here?' And the doctors weren't much better. They were impatient, always in a hurry. 'There's nothing wrong,' they'd say, 'go home and try again.' One told me it was all in my head, that I really didn't *want* to have a baby. Another one said I should just accept it. One so-called friend, who had three children herself, told me the world was overpopulated anyway. I used to cry a lot."

So did a lot of other women who, like Mrs. D., have since become pregnant and given birth to healthy children, thanks to a number of exciting medical advances and the slow-but-sure emergence of a new breed of doctors compassionately concerned about the problems of the infertile. It is conservatively estimated that there are 3.5 million couples in the United States who are unable to have children and an additional 2.5 million couples who have substantial difficulty in conceiving or carrying a child to term. (Generally, a couple that has tried to have a child for two years without success is considered infertile.)

Here, then, is a sizable minority, embracing some twelve million Americans. It is a minority that is, in this era of birth control, The Pill and the Population Explosion, too often forgotten or simply dismissed as "unimportant."

"Our heavy emphasis on birth control," says Dr. Albert C. Decker, an internationally known researcher in the field of human reproduction, "has unfortunately led some doctors to believe that they have no real obligation to try to cope with infertility. 'Oh, well,' they say, 'why should we bother about this?' But another group of doctors, and one that is growing, recognizes how unfair it is to tell a woman, 'Forget about it, somebody else will have the babies for you.' We must remember that motherhood is a complex emotional thing, not just an institution." These sentiments are echoed by two other pioneering researchers, who have been active in the study of contraception as well as infertility and hence know both sides of the story. "These couples should not be denied the right to have children simply because others have too many," says Dr. Martin J. Clyman, associate clinical professor of obstetrics and gynecology at New York's Mount Sinai School of Medicine. "A doctor is just as obligated to help a patient who wants to have children as he is to help those who don't want them or who don't want to have any more," adds Dr. Maxwell Roland, director of the non-profit New York Fertility Research Foundation (where Mrs. D. finally got help).

Encouraging as these attitudes are, is there really substantial evidence that the situation is improving? Yes. Dr. Decker, on the staff of several New York hospitals and a professor at New York Medical College, says, "Twenty years ago when I tried to organize a group of doctors interested in sterility only five showed up. At a recent professional gathering in Miami, 3000 doctors concerned with the problem were in attendance." And Dr. Clyman states flatly that "the infertile woman has a 50 per cent better chance of getting pregnant now than she did just ten years ago."

Underlying this phenomenal improvement, says

Dr. Roland, author of a book for doctors called *Management of the Infertile Couple,* are advances in diagnostic, medical and surgical procedures, as well as recognition on the part of physicians that "the infertile are people, too." Ironically, Dr. Roland notes, "It has been the inquiry into methods of *preventing* pregnancy that has given us some very valuable insights into the fundamental causes and treatment of infertility." The Pill itself is now being used to treat endometriosis, one of the commonest causes of infertility. Other remarkable new drugs are promising many women who do not ovulate at all or who ovulate improperly a chance for the first time to become pregnant. A strange phenomenon, involving "immunity" on the part of some women to their husbands' sperm, is now coming under close scrutiny and in many cases yielding to successful treatment. A revolutionary and simple diagnostic technique known as "culdoscopy" is permitting doctors to look inside the pelvis, examine and even take motion pictures of the ovaries, uterus and fallopian tubes in a matter of minutes without having to cut open the abdomen. Some cases of infertility that were regarded as hopeless only a few years ago are now being successfully treated with bold surgical reconstruction of damaged tubes. Frozen-sperm banks and artificial insemination (sometimes using the "pooled" sperm of the husband rather than of some anonymous donor) are contributing to still other successful pregnancies.

In the future, tubal and ovarian transplants, though far more complex than any heart transplant, may be possible. Even more likely for the Brave New World of tomorrow are embryo implants, to be used in women whose tubes simply cannot be repaired. If a woman is able, however, to produce viable eggs these could be extracted and inseminated with her husband's sperm outside the womb—then implanted. If she does not ovulate at all, then another woman's egg cell would have to be used; but at least the infertile woman in whom the embryo is implanted will be able to experience the joy and fulfillment of carrying and giving birth to a baby. Some of the ramifications of this procedure (including its possible application to women who do not have fertlity problems) are discussed in more detail in the next chapter.

One of the most significant advances in the treatment of the infertile, though one that has not been widely utilized yet, embraces a simple principle, namely that a troublesome disorder such as infertility (which can have its roots in the husband as well as the wife, in the psychological as well as the physical) can be most quickly, most efficiently and, in the long run, most economically treated by a group of specialists gathered under one roof.

To illustrate, let's take Lynda's case. After a June wedding, she and Bob decided to start raising a family right away. "Our parents were old and gray when we were in our teens," says Lynda, "and we didn't want that to happen to our children. It was none of that career-first business for us." Or so they thought. The months went by, and Lynda did not become pregnant. "Embarrassing as it was, I finally went to my family doctor," she recalls. "He gave me a routine physical and sent me home, saying everything was fine." She went back to this doctor intermittently for a year, but with no better results.

At no point during this phase of the "quest" was it suggested that Bob be examined, as well. And, of course, most husbands resist such examinations, egotistically assuming that they couldn't possibly be the "guilty" parties. This attitude dates back to biblical times when women who could not produce children were regarded as outcasts. Literally thousands of men have divorced or abandoned their wives, even in recent times, because they did not bring them children —only to discover later, in many cases, that they were themselves infertile. Indeed, fully 35 per cent of all infertility today is attributed to males whose sperm quality or count is inadequate for the fertilizing task. Male infertility, unlike female infertility, can usually be determined in a matter of minutes, simply by examing sperm specimens under the microscope. Yet, many doctors fail to apprise their patients of this, perhaps because, being men in most cases, they share the male prejudice that most infertility is due to some shortcoming on the part of the female.

As it turned out, Bob was not responsible for the infertility, but this was not revealed until Lynda sought out a second doctor, an obstetrician recommended by a friend. Unfortunately, this doctor could not find anything wrong with Lynda, either. She seemed to be ovulating normally, which was enough to satisfy him. "I got the feeling," she says, "that he didn't know what to do with me. Neither did the next doctor I went to. None of them wanted to give up time delivering babies to work on my case. I was only too willing to cooperate, to do everything they suggested. But they couldn't suggest a thing—except that I see another doctor at a place called the New York Fertility Research Foundation.

"By this time we were considering adoption, but after three years of going from one doctor to another we figured it wouldn't hurt to try once more, which by this time had almost become our motto. I don't know what it was, but when we walked into the Foundation (in Manhattan) we just knew everything was going to be different." Mrs. D., the woman who "used to cry a lot," registered a similar reaction on her first visit to the Foundation and thinks she knows why: "All the women in the waiting room have flat tummies, just like you do," she observes wryly. "For the first time, you feel that somebody else understands your problem."

Lynda's problem was understood—and quickly. "A few months after I went through those doors I was pregnant. I was so happy I forgot to be bitter about all those other years and all those other doctors." What happened at the Foundation was this: The couple was immediately assigned to one of the many highly experienced doctors who staff the clinic. He immediately had a urologist examine Bob, who got a clean bill of health. Then he ran a battery of tests on Lynda—not over a period of months, but immediately. When these failed to reveal anything wrong, the doctor did not send her home or treat her like a psychiatric case. (It was evident to him, after lengthy discussions with Bob and Lynda together, and then separately, that no sexual incompatibility or psychological barriers to pregnancy existed; if they had, he could have called in one of the Foundation's psychiatrists who are specially trained in "psychosomatic infertility.") Instead, the doctor ordered a culdoscopic examination.

"That worried me a little," Lynda admits, "because they said it was a surgical procedure. As it turned out, I was only in the hospital one night and didn't have any pain during or after the procedure, even though it was performed with only a local anesthetic." The operation involves puncturing a very thin septum of skin called the cul-de-sac, which is next to the cervix and is accessible through the vagina, thus necessitating no surgical incision. The puncture in the cul-de-sac is so minor that it does not even result in any bleeding and subsequently requires no suturing. It is through this aperture that a pencil-like culdoscope is introduced.

The scope is simply a viewing device with an eyepiece at one end and a lens and light at the other. The light, however, is not of any conventional nature. In place of a bulb, which would burn the patient painfully, the culdoscope utilizes thousands of tiny hollow fibers through which light is channeled from an external source. In this way, tremendous amounts of "cool" light can be projected into the pelvis, more than enough to provide clear vision of the uterus, tubes and ovaries. These can be viewed through the scope with the naked eye or through still and motion-picture cameras attached to the external end of the scope. In Lynda's case, one glance with the naked eye was enough to tell the doctor that she was suffering from endometriosis, which had partially blocked her tubes. (There are other ways of trying to determine whether the tubes are blocked but results are considered faulty about 50 per cent of the time.)

Dr. Decker, who recently won the coveted Gold Medal of the Barren Foundation for his development of the culdoscope, which is now being used in large clinics all around the world, estimates that "at least 20 per cent of all problem cases of infertility are due to endometriosis which, if not caught in its early stages, is one of the most sterilizing conditions we know of." Some women harbor the notion that endometriosis is a form of cancer. This is not true; it isn't even an infection. Its main effect, as Dr. Decker puts it, is to "gum up the works." As in Lynda's case, it can cause the tubes to stick together and thus close up, preventing the egg from migrating into the uterus.

The material doing the "gumming" is similar to the tissue that lines the uterus. This lining is called endometrium, and that's where the disease gets its name. The endometrium goes through cyclic stages each month. It builds itself up as ovulation approaches, making a soft, receptive bed for the fertilized egg cell. If no fertilized egg arrives (and, of course, most months none does), it tears itself down and the waste is extruded during menstruation. Then the cycle starts over again.

In the individual afflicted with endometriosis, this cyclic pattern occurs not only in the uterus but also wherever these bits and pieces of endometrium-like material have attached themselves, which, all too often, is on the tubes and ovaries. The material grows and bleeds each month in the pelvic areas and wastes pile up. The blood congeals and forms distinctive "chocolate cysts" that are immediately identifiable through the culdoscope.

What causes this bizarre disease is not yet fully understood. Dr. Decker believes it results from failure of a mechanism in the fallopian tubes that normally prevents endometrium material from draining into the tubes and pelvic cavity at the time of menstruation. An alternate explanation, called the "embryonic-remnant theory," maintains that these pieces are scattered about, perhaps by some genetic error, during the embryonic stage of a woman's development. Then the disease lies dormant until the baby grows into a girl and begins menstruating. It builds up through the teens and becomes a serious problem in the twenties and thirties.

The most common symptom is pain at time of menstruation. "Unfortunately," Dr. Decker says, "too many mothers tell their daughters that this is just part of growing up. Nonsense. Any girl who has painful menstruation should see a doctor at once." He concedes, however, that this sometimes does no good. "Too many doctors, when faced with unexplained pelvic pain, simply take the patient's appendix out—and the pain goes right on. We've somehow got to make more doctors aware of this problem."

Further complicating matters, Dr. Clyman points out, is the fact that endometriosis can be "occult," meaning that even complex tubal X rays cannot detect it. This, he says, is true in more than a quarter of all the cases that are finally confirmed by culdoscopic examination. And though there are no symptoms, the damage in these cases is usually sufficient to result in infertility.

This was true in Lynda's case. Without culdoscopy her endometriosis might never have been detected—or only detected so late that large portions of the ovaries and tubes would have to be cut out, probably ruling out any chance of her ever having a child. In fact, until recently, even relatively mild cases of endometriosis had to be treated surgically. Now, again as in Lynda's case, it is very often controlled, and in mild cases cured, by simple use of the birth-control pill. The Pill suppresses the normal cycle of ovulation and causes activity in these stray pieces of endometrium to diminish and sometimes die out completely, thus freeing up the system so that it can function in the normal way once The Pill is withdrawn. Even in more severe cases, The Pill can sometimes clean up the system long enough for pregnancy to occur before the tubes are clogged again.

In cases where the tubes and ovaries are so badly agglutinated that medication is useless, there is still hope. Surgery in these cases is required, but the results are often gratifying. Affected areas of the tubes are cut out and the remaining portions stitched together. To keep the passageways open until healing can take place, inert Teflon tubing is implanted. The tubing extends out a puncture in the abdomen after the operation, so that it can be removed, usually six weeks later, without reopening the abdomen. It is simply pulled out very gently. Dr. Clyman has performed some four hundred of these operations and has achieved pregnancies in about 21 per cent of the cases.

Recently, he developed a technique known as "operative culdoscopy." He has devised special surgical tools that can be introduced, along with the culdoscope, through the vagina and into the pelvic area, permitting on-the-spot surgery under local anesthesia and without any abdominal incision! He can even pull the tubes right into the vaginal vault where they are easier to repair. This technique, he says, could double his fertility rate—besides sparing his patients major surgery.

There are many women, of course, who have perfectly functioning tubes but faulty ovaries. Some do not ovulate at all. There was very little, if anything, that could be done for these women until a powerful hormone drug called Clomid was cleared for use in this country in 1967. Now a similar but possibly even more potent drug called Pergonal is coming into use. Both of these compounds stimulate the follicles of the ovaries, inducing them to release eggs they hold captive. Pergonal was first produced by a pharmacological company in Rome, and the active ingredient—the follicle-stimulating hormone (FSH)—was gathered and purified from the urine of post-menopausal women (all of whom were nuns). Post-menopausal women are used since their pituitary glands produce an abundance of FSH that is no longer used by the body and so is excreted into the urine. Some 25 per cent of the three thousand infertile women treated in clinical trials with daily injections of this new drug (for five to ten days) became pregnant, Dr. Clyman reports.

Occasionally, Dr. Roland says, even specialists in the treatment of infertility have come up against cases that could not be explained with the most exhaustive diagnostic techniques, including culdoscopy. But now this "black area" of unexplained infertility is lighting up, too. Between 40 and 60 per cent of the cases that previously fell into this category are now believed caused by women who develop antibodies that war against their husbands' sperm, just as if it were some foreign body that must be destroyed like any other infectious invader. Why this happens in some women and not in others isn't understood, but a number of simple tests have been devised now to detect the presence of such antibodies, and treatment is not at all complex. The wife's antibodies build up in number in direct proportion to the amount of sperm she is exposed to. Hence, Dr. Roland explains, the husband is simply instructed in these cases to use a condom during intercourse until the antibody count is negligible. This usually takes from one to twelve months, after which pregnancies are achieved in more than 40 per cent of these previously "unexplainable" cases.

Still other cases that appear for a time to be unexplainable turn out to have psychological origins. While recognizing this fact, some doctors caution against giving the psychological factor more weight than it deserves, pointing out that too many physicians have, in the past, used the "all-in-your-head" approach to brush off infertility patients they couldn't cope with. But with care, the psychological factors can be distinguished from the physical.

Doctors experienced in the treatment of infertility are always on the lookout for emotional factors that might cause impotence, premature ejaculation and retrograde ejaculation (in which the sperm is propelled backward instead of forward) in men and tubal spasms, frigidity preventing adequate sperm migration and even lack of ovulation in women. It has been well established that all of these conditions can be due to psychic stress. Fear is often an underlying factor and sometimes it is so overriding that the individual will consciously avoid pregnancy even while going to a doctor for the expressed purpose of achieving it. This sort of confused and confusing deception poses formidable problems for the physician and, according to Dr. Roland, is far commoner than one might expect.

He relates the case of a thirty-two-year-old woman who had been married for eight years when she first consulted him. "She reported that she had unsuccessfully attempted to have a child for the last seven years of her marriage. Previously, four physicians had tried to help her to no avail." Dr. Roland could discover nothing wrong with the woman or her husband—physically. It was only through long, painstaking sessions with this patient that he got an inkling of her real problem.

It seemed that the woman's father had abandoned her mother after she was born. Dr. Roland suspected, of course, that his patient feared the same treatment from her own husband, in the event of the birth of a child. Finally he elicited a full confession. "She admitted that she took a douche after each intercourse and kept a record to avoid intercourse during the fertile portion of each monthly cycle. She kept going to doctors only to convince her husband of her eagerness for a child." This simple opening-up helped her overcome her fears and a few months later she conceived.

Not all psychological cases are this easy—or have such happy endings. In cases where the doctor suspects that *unconscious* fears are at work, Dr. Roland cautions, a psychiatrist should be called in. Dr. Roland had one patient who sought his help (after six years of infertility) and after hormone therapy became pregnant and bore a healthy child, only to withdraw immediately into a near psychotic state. It took four years of intensive psychoanalysis to learn that this patient never really wanted a child due to an unconscious fear of childbirth that resulted from the near death of her mother while giving birth to the patient. (The mother spoke of this during later years —in the presence of her daughter.) Psychological stress often causes a patient's system to habitually abort fetuses during their earliest development. What this boils down to, Dr. Roland explains, is that "psychogenic infertility may represent an essential means for maintaining a person's psychological equilibrium." In other words, pregnancy, though desirable in most cases, is definitely not good for everyone.

Sometimes no amount of physical and psychological treatment can result in pregnancy—for the simple reason that the husband either produces no sperm whatever or sperm of such inadequate quantity and quality that that fertilization is not possible. In borderline cases, where sperm count is low but not prohibitively low, some pregnancies have been achieved by "splitting" the semen ejaculate. Studies show that sperm count is significantly higher in the first half of the ejaculate than in the second. The first half of a husband's sperm, in these cases, can be used to artificially inseminate his wife, often with success. Where this doesn't work, doctors usually have no option left but to recommend artificial insemination using sperm from an anonymous donor. This method of acquiring a child is often preferred to adoption, for both genetic and psychological reasons. Artificial insemination now accounts for the births of more than ten thousand healthy babies in the United States each year.

Half a dozen frozen-sperm banks are already in existence and these may proliferate in the near future. "The advantage here," Dr. Clyman explains, "is that a better parent-child match can be achieved." Doctors try to select donors who resemble their patients but this is not always possible. Large frozen-sperm banks, complete with detailed catalogues, are expected to provide opportunities for excellent matches. Freezing techniques will also be used to store the sperm of men whose count is very low, using it for insemination when enough has been collected and concentrated.

For the future, tubal and even ovarian transplants may also be in the cards, Dr. Clyman says, provided that we someday find an effective drug to counter the rejection phenomenon. A woman with implanted ovaries would give birth to children in the normal fashion, but the real, biological mother in this case would be the donor of the ovaries, which produce only one set of eggs. An even more utopian approach to the problem of infertility—and several other "problems" as well—is discussed in the next chapter.

# TWO

# Embryo Implants: A Startling New Way to Have a Baby

The techniques about to be described have not, at this writing, been applied to man. They have, however, been used very successfully with animals, and doctors are, at this moment, poised for their first attempts to apply the procedures to human patients. So project yourself into the future a few months and imagine a woman whom we shall call Mrs. Smith.

Mrs. Smith is thirty, a young, ambitious woman of ample means. Her career demands that she constantly be before the public and that she constantly look her best. Yet, like most women, she longs to have children and have them while she is still young. There is no biological reason why she can't have children; she simply doesn't want to incapacitate herself those long months during pregnancy.

A friend tells Mrs. Smith about a new medical "miracle" that can solve her problem. Though Mrs. Smith is a little shocked at what her friend tells her she decides, after some reflection and numerous discussions with her husband (who is even more shocked than she), that it really is the answer to her problem and not at all the "unnatural" thing she thought at first.

So, after a chat with the doctor recommended by her friend, Mrs. Smith goes off contraceptives briefly and becomes pregnant. Two or three days after conception, Mrs. Smith goes back to her doctor, who flushes from her body the tiny speck of life that is already rapidly developing within her. The doctor places the fertilized egg in a carefully prepared nutrient bath while he gets ready to implant it into the womb of another woman (whom we will call Mrs. Jones). The doctor takes care to see that both Mrs. Smith and Mrs. Jones are in the same stage of their monthly cycles. In addition, he injects Mrs. Jones with a number of hormone preparations. All of this helps ensure a hospitable reception for the nearly microscopic embryo in its new environment. Once Mrs. Jones has undergone the implantation procedure Mrs. Smith pays her a pre-arranged fee. And that's that. Nine months later the Smiths go to the hospital to pick up their baby, and Mrs. Jones gets her final payment.

Horrifying? Before deciding, consider these variations on the preceding scenario:

In this case, let us assume that Mrs. Smith is an entirely different woman—a typical suburban housewife. Typical, except for one thing. Though she and her husband have been married eight years, they have no children. The strange part about this is that neither Mr. nor Mrs. X is sterile. Why then have they remained childless? Because, like thousands of other women throughout the United States, Mrs. X has a physical condition that might be dangerously aggravated by the rigors of pregnancy. That condition could be any of a number of ills, but in her case it is the most typical of them: chronic heart disease.

Mrs. Smith can lead a normal life—up to a point. She can conceive a child. And if she doesn't overwork herself there is no reason why she can't raise children. But her doctor has warned time and again it would be foolhardy of her to try to bear a child. Yet, this same doctor now advises her that, even though there has been no change in her heart condition, it is suddenly possible for her to have a child of her own, thanks to the new embryo-implantation procedure.

This time, instead of hiring someone to carry the baby for her, Mrs. Smith prevails upon a sister to receive the embryo. Mrs. Smith's sister is unmarried, and the doctor is reluctant at first to use her in the procedure. But then he decides there is nothing at all wrong with this. He reasons that the birth, when it comes, will really be a sort of "virgin birth." During the next nine months, of course, Mrs. Smith and her sister are inseparable. When the sister feels the baby first beginning to kick, Mrs. Smith is as excited as if it were happening to herself. And she can hardly blame her husband for lavishing so much attention on her sister, even when he calls her in the middle of the night to make sure everything is all right. During periodic checkups during the nine months, Mrs. Smith is right there in the examining room with her sister, and both Smiths are present during delivery, after which they thank the sister and take possession of their baby.

Somewhat better, you're thinking, though the sister still gets the short end of the stick. True, but remember that the sister will be able to have children of her own later on. And meanwhile she has very unselfishly helped Mrs. Smith have one of *her* own, something previously impossible without considerable risk to her health. The procedure has still other possibilities, which are revealed in the next two "case histories":

Mrs. Smith, instead of having a heart condition, in this case has not been able to have children because her oviducts are partially blocked by some malformation. The oviducts are the tubes that lead from the ovaries to the womb, and it is in one or the other of them that fertilization takes place. A significant proportion of infertility results from irregularities and blockage of these tubes. In Mrs. Smith's case, the blockage does not prevent fertilization of the egg, but it does prevent the fertilized egg from passing all the way down into the uterus where it would normally attach itself and grow into a normal baby. Hence, Mrs. Smith has failed for years to become pregnant.

This time it isn't necessary to bring in another woman to carry Mrs. Smith's embryo. There is no reason why Mrs. Smith cannot carry the baby herself. The problem is simply one of getting Mrs. Smith's ferilized egg into her uterus. The doctor removes Mrs. Smith's egg—*before* fertilization—and exposes it to Mr. Smith's sperm in a test tube. Once fertilization has taken place in this fashion, the doctor implants the embryo in Mrs. Smith's womb and lets nature take her course. Thus a woman who was diagnosed for years as infertile abruptly proves otherwise.

Mrs. Smith, in this final vignette, is indeed sterile. She is completely unable to produce viable eggs. Otherwise, however, she is healthy and, given the opportunity, could easily carry a baby to term. She and her husband, in considerable anguish over their situation, think about adopting a child. Mrs. Smith, however, does not feel psychologically equipped to face the uncertainties of adoption. Moreover, like many women, she has an overpowering desire to bear a child herself, even if it isn't biologically her own. When she hears about the egg-implantation technique, which makes possible a sort of "prenatal adoption," she is determined to try it.

Like those obstetricians and gynecologists who specialize in artificial insemination, the doctor Mrs. Smith goes to has an anonymous panel of donors. But in this case the donors consist of married couples who provide embryos for implantation rather than of single men, in the case of artificial insemination, who provide sperm. The couples have been selected by Mrs. Smith's doctor for their physical, mental and genetic superiority. The doctor selects the couple that most resembles Mr. and Mrs. Smith, not only in physical appearance but in attitude, personality and, if requested, even religion.

At no time do Mr. and Mrs. Smith themselves actually see the donor couple; nor are they ever apprised of the name of the donor couple. By the same token, the donors do not know who they are donating to; they simply provide their genetic material anonymously—for a fee, which is paid by the patients to the doctor and then to the donors.

A schedule is arranged to provide for proper timing, and when the moment comes, the embryo produced by the donor couple is implanted into the uterus of Mrs. Smith, who carries it to term and raises the child as if it were biologically her own. She knows, of course, that she and her husband have contributed nothing to the child's genetic makeup but at least she has enjoyed the fulfilling experience of childbirth despite the fact that she is "hopelessly sterile." She has the satisfaction, too, of knowing that the child she brings into the world, thanks to the careful screening procedures of her doctor, will almost certainly be healthy and of above-average intelligence.

It may be slightly optimistic to suppose that experiences such as these will be commonplace within the next few years. But there is no question that egg and embryo implants will be applied to humans soon. These procedures are already being utilized routinely —and very profitably—in cattle and other mammals. Their promise for mankind is both great and, from the standpoint of the past, somewhat bizarre.

Five years ago, if anyone had even suggested that we were on the verge of an era in which a sterile woman could give birth to a child conceived by another woman or a woman could hire a "mother surrogate" to have her child for her, many scientists would have responded with disbelief. Now, Dr. Kurt Hirschhorn, chief of the Division of Medical Genetics at the Mount Sinai School of Medicine in New York, says, "There is no question whatever in my mind that all of this is going to happen."

Indeed, as major medical developments go, progress has proceeded at a phenomenal rate. It was only twelve years ago that a group of researchers at Cambridge began investigating the possibility of transferring eggs from one animal to another. Livestock breeders became interested almost immediately, particularly since they knew that all animals (including humans) produce far more eggs than they ever use. The Cambridge team discovered that if they injected FSH, a hormone that prompts follicles in the ovaries to release eggs, into cows the animals would undergo mass ovulation, releasing up to one hundred eggs at a time.

After artificially inseminating the best cows with the sperm of prize bulls, the researchers waited a few days and then implanted the pea-size embryos into other healthy, but less exalted, cows. And while the mother surrogates grew heavy with their burdens, the real mothers gamboled freely, preparing to conceive new sets of prize centuplets.

It is true that the human reproductive processes are somewhat more complex than those of cattle. But many scientists believe that a doctor with the requisite patience—and boldness—could apply these techniques to human patients right now with considerable success. The procedure involves little or no risk for the patient; but since it concerns the most intimate processes of life, it is going to be controversial. Many doctors have not forgotten the storm that whirled around artificial insemination when it was introduced to the public. Yet today artificial insemination, once exclusively for ranch and farm, accounts for several thousand healthy human babies each year.

One doctor apparently ready to brave the storm is Patrick Steptoe, a leading British gynecologist. Dr. Steptoe recently appeared on television with one of his patients, a thirty-four-year-old woman who was unable to become pregnant, like one of our Mrs. Smiths, because of blocked fallopian tubes. Dr. Steptoe, during the interview, said that he had removed one of his patient's eggs and then had fertilized it in his laboratory with sperm from the woman's husband. He did not indicate when he would try to reimplant the egg but indicated that even if he failed on this first attempt he felt that he would ultimately succeed.

The minor operation to remove the egg from the ovary, he said, "causes very little disturbance in the woman, and she should completely recover in less than twenty-four hours." At last report, Dr. Steptoe reported that he had some fifty childless women waiting to have the operation, once it is perfected.

It is evident that artificial inovulation is about to enjoy the same evolution—from curiosity to clinical procedure—that artificial insemination did. But its impact is going to be far more important than that of artificial insemination. And together the two techniques are expected to revolutionize our century-old notions about reproduction.

To begin with, they will at last make possible—and hence inevitably promote—the concept of germinal choice that was discussed in the Introduction. Controversial as this program for improving the human race seems—by inseminating women only with the sperm of genetically superior men—it has attracted wide support. The plan, if ever implemented, would probably be run by the government or a government-licensed agency and would involve strict screening of donors and the issuance of permits to recipients. Dr. F. H. C. Crick, a Nobel Prize-winning molecular biologist, explains his favorable attitude toward the program by saying that having children "is at least as much a matter of public interest as having a license to drive a car."

Dr. Muller lived to see the widespread use of artificial insemination in man and even the establishment of several frozen-sperm banks across the country. He predicted the imminent use of egg and embryo implants, noting that these breakthroughs would make possible a complete program of germinal choice, wherein parents could "construct" their child not only of the best sperm available but also of the best eggs. In sharp contrast to current policies of absolute donor anonymity, Dr. Muller called for detailed descriptions of all egg and sperm donors and proposed that these be made available to prospective parents so that they could make a wise decision. He envisioned catalogues that the prospective parents could flip through in search of the ideal egg to be mated with the ideal sperm. Presumably, these catalogues would contain not only vivid verbal descriptions of the donors' mental and physical characteristics but would also include their pictures. Color, of course. And it seems likely that each human entry would be cross-referenced in such a way that it would be impossible to match genetically incompatible sex cells with one another. The cross-referencing—which might appear in the form of a numerical code that could be translated with the help of tables at the back of the catalogue—could also be used to help parents-to-be get a tailor-made baby, perfect (in terms of their personal taste) in every detail. A number 7793-Y sperm matched with a number 3083-X egg, for example, might be guaranteed, ultimately to produce a blue-eyed, blond-haired boy of medium build—with a light spattering of freckles.

Dr. E. S. E. Hafez, an experimental biologist at Washington State University and one of the world's foremost researchers in this new field, foresees the day, perhaps only ten or fifteen years hence, when a wife can stroll through a special kind of market and select her baby from a wide selection of one-day-old *frozen* embryos, guaranteed free of all genetic defects and described, as to sex, eye color, probable IQ, and so on, in detail on the labels. A color picture of what the grown-up product is likely to resemble, he says, could also be included on the outside of the packet. Following the purchase, the embryo would be thawed out and implanted under a doctor's supervision.

Dr. Hafez has been working on the problems of preserving embryos and has hit upon two successful techniques. When it is only necesssary to preserve cattle embryos for a short period of time, he sometimes places them—using a minor surgical procedure—in the oviducts of smaller animals such as rabbits. In this unlikely environment, the tiny cow embryos go on growing normally for as long as fourteen days. This remarkable technique, Dr. Hafez notes, makes it possible to transport a whole herd of prize cattle across the ocean or around the world inside a single rabbit—a tiny, economical package, indeed! After being removed from the rabbit, they are simply implanted in other cows and carried through to term, leaving the prize mother once again free to go on producing more prize eggs without taking time out for pregnancy. In this way, a superior cow can "mother" hundreds of calves instead of the ten or twelve she would normally be limited to, if she had to endure the rigors of pregnancy herself.

For long-range preservation, Dr. Hafez is experimenting with freezing of embryos. This may seem a little far-fetched, but remember that sperm has already been kept in the deep freeze for up to ten-year periods and when thawed has still been capable of fertilizing eggs. Though this phase of Dr. Hafez' work is still in its infancy, he already reports keeping animal embryos frozen for periods of up to twelve days, after which he has successfully thawed them out still alive. Ultimately, Dr. Hafez believes, entire colonies of men and animals can be contained in small, frozen packages and launched to distant planets, along with a few fully grown scientists and mother surrogates.

The idea, apart from its Buck Rogers charm, has a great deal to commend itself, particularly in terms of economics. The cost of sending one hundred frozen embryos across the vast expanses of space would certainly be only a fraction of what it would cost to send one hundred fully grown men and women. Fuel is only one of the considerations; more important, in terms of dollars and cents, are the life-support systems that could be minimized on a spaceship freighted with frozen embryos. And there is the added advan-

tage that the embryos would not, for all practical purposes, be a day older when they arrived at their
destination than when they left; nor would they be in
any way vulnerable to boredom, a problem that could
reach ominous proportions on some of the long space-
flights already contemplated.

Of course, not all the scientists are so optimistic as
Dr. Hafez. Some fear that the techniques of artificial
insemination and embryo implantation may be mis-
used or that society may fail to make the necessary
adjustments. Almost certainly, like so many other scientific advances, these will give rise to a number of
agonizing moral and ethical questions, some of which
will have to be resolved in the courts.

What will happen, for example, when a hired
mother surrogate refuses to give up a child she has
carried and nurtured for nine months? Even though
she has no real, biological claim on the child, having
contributed nothing to its genetic makeup, might she
not present some persuasive emotional claim? She,
after all, has risked her life, giving of her body and
blood for nine months. Might not some courts consider
the claims of the real parents, in such a case, feeble at
best, noting that they contributed only a few minutes
(during intercourse) to the total effort required to
bring new life into the world?

On the other hand, what will society do about the
woman who for reasons of health or cancer has her
embryo implanted in another woman but then refuses
to accept it when it is finally born? Such cases are
bound to arise; some women, with good intentions to
begin with, will inevitably find that they are psychologically unable to accept children borne by other
women, even though these children are biologically
their own. Probably this will not happen in too many
cases, but when it does occur it will be tragic not only
for the adults involved but even more so for the child.

There are other, more complex questions to be
ironed out—preferably *before* these techniques become widespread. What will happen in cases where

the "anonymity" of the donors of the embryos breaks down, where either recipient or donor discovers the identity of the other. Donors, no matter how carefully screened, are human, too. It seems likely that some of them will be sufficiently curious about their "farmed out" offspring to ultimately seek them out and possibly make known their true parentage. One needn't dwell on the trauma this could inflict on the children involved. But consider, in addition, the possibility that some of the donors might, after locating their flesh and blood, seek possession of them—in the same way that many unwed mothers later seek possession of a child so hastily given up for adoption. What then?

Not all the difficulties, of course, would have to originate with the donors. Recipients of embryos, if somehow disappointed with the resulting child, might conceivably seek out the donors and insist that they take the child back. Or if the recipient obtained her embryo from a national, computerized and catalogued embryo bank, of the sort envisioned by Drs. Muller and Hafez, carrying with it certain "guarantees" against defects and so on, other problems could arise. If a boy were promised and a girl resulted or if brown eyes were advertised and blue eyes turned up, should the parents be entitled to an exchange or a "refund"? And if so, what would happen to the unwanted child, the "reject," as it were? Would it be placed on sale— at "cut rate"? One hopes not, of course, but these are all things that should and in fact *must* be given serious consideration before the problems arise.

And the potential problems go on and on. If a child resulting from an embryo implant, to cite yet another example, discovers the identity of his real biological parents, what claim, if any, could he make upon them? Could he conceivably sue them for denying him their presence, their love, for *selling* him? Or in the event of an estate proceeding could he claim to be a legal heir?

When it becomes possible to store human embryos for long periods of time new problems will crop up.

Inevitably there will be couples who will want to put one or more embryos into "safekeeping" in the deep freeze, perhaps as "spares" to be used in the event that something happens to their other children at a point when they themselves are beyond the ideal reproductive age. Some may go so far as to stipulate in their wills, if such is permitted, that their stored embryos be thawed out and implanted in hirelings after their deaths, as an indirect means of perpetuating themselves.

It was Dr. Jean Rostand, the famed French biologist, who predicted that man, before very long, would have to adjust to the notion that children can be born to parents who have been long dead or separated by continents or even planets their entire lives, to parents who have not even necessarily seen one another—*ever*. With the arrival of artificial insemination, embryo implantation, egg and sperm banks and fertilization of eggs outside the womb, that time is already at hand. No one can yet predict with any certainty what the psychological effects of "telegenesis" (the creation of life achieved by the comingling of two sex cells obtained from points distant in space) and "paleogenesis" (life generated from two sex cells obtained at different points in time or at the same time but well in advance of birth) will be on the brave new babies of tomorrow. But it does seem highly probable that there *will be* far-reaching effects.

None of these problems, however, is insurmountable, and if society will act in time to circumvent the peril it will endure to reap the promise of these great advances.

# THREE

# Selecting the Sex of Your Baby

Over the centuries, man has devised at least five hundred "formulas" to help satisfy his overwhelming desire to choose the sex of his offspring. Aristotle advised the Greeks to have intercourse in the north wind if males were desired, in the south wind whenever females were wanted. Women of the Middle Ages didn't get off so easily. When boys were desired, they were required to down gamy concoctions of wine and lion's blood mixed by an alchemist and then, while an abbot prayed, to copulate under a full moon. When girls resulted despite these heroics, local wise men were usually ready with obscure "explanations." Some European peasants to this day wear their boots to bed when they want to conceive boys, and in some rural American communities men still hang their pants on the right side of the bed if they want a boy and on the left side if they want a girl.

Interest in choosing sex remains as high among prospective parents today as it ever was, perhaps much higher since we have come to expect so much of modern medicine. And failure to produce the desired sex still creates as much anguish as it did in the past. As one young housewife from Virginia who has three boys put it, "My doctor said I was being silly and immature when I begged him to help me have a little girl. He has children of both sexes and can't understand the deep hurt of having children of the same sex over and over."

One doctor who does understand the anguish of such parents—and has set out to do something about it—is Landrum B. Shettles, M.D., Ph.D., D.Sc., a gynecologist at Columbia-Presbyterian Medical Center and a faculty member at the Columbia College of Physicians and Surgeons in New York City. A few years ago he made a discovery that he now believes can help millions of people select the sex of their offspring.

"Medical science had known for some time," he says, "that it is the male that determines the sex of the offspring. The man who leaves his wife because she brings him nothing but girls is only kidding himself. If the man's fertilizing sperm carries an X chromosome, the child will be a girl; if it carries a Y, the child will be a boy."

The trouble was, he adds, doctors had always been unable to tell the difference between "male" sperm and "female" sperm. About all that was known was that the Y chromosome is smaller than the X. Dr. Shettles had felt for a long time that this difference should be reflected in the overall size of the sperm heads. Using ordinary microscopy, however, Dr. Shettles was unable to detect the presence to two distinct sperm populations among killed and permanently fixed specimens.

"Then one night," Dr. Shettles recalls, "I decided to examine some *living* sperm cells under a phase-contrast microscope." This relatively new technique throws eerie halos of light around dark objects, revealing details that ordinary microscopes miss. The living sperm cells flashed through the field of vision like luminescent eels. Dr. Shettles put them into slow motion by exposing them to carbon dioxide gas. The results were almost as electrifying as the "charged" sperm cells themselves: almost immediately, Dr. Shettles noticed that the sperm came in two distinct sizes and shapes.

"I was so excited," he says, "that I ran upstairs and grabbed the first lab technician I could find. I had to show somebody what I had found."

Now, after examining more than five hundred sperm specimens, he is convinced that the two sizes correspond to the two sexes: small, round-headed sperm carry the male-producing Y chromosomes, and the larger, oval-shaped type carry the female-producing X chromosomes. He noticed that in most cases the round sperm far outnumbered the oval-shaped sperm.

Dr. Shettles failed to find anyone who produced only the oval-shaped female sperm, but he did encounter some men whose specimens contained almost nothing but the round-headed variety. In each of the latter cases, his physiological sleuthing revealed a man who had produced nothing but male offspring. In cases in which the long-headed sperm prevailed, he generally found fathers surrounded by little girls (and wives who wanted boys).

Dr. Shettles stresses here, however, the rarity of cases in which the husband produces sperm that is predominantly of one type. And even in cases in which a man may produce unusually more sperm of one type than of the other, he can very often still produce offspring of both sexes, provided he follows certain procedures. Individuals who have repeatedly fathered children of the same sex are more often the victims of bad luck than of genetics.

After making his discovery, Dr. Shettles published his findings in the scientific journal *Nature*. Not everybody agreed with his conclusions, and he does not claim scientific infallibility. But he does stand on his record, on his laboratory observations and, most important, on his results to date. Other researchers, moreover, have provided some impressive corroboration of his work.

As soon as he had made his initial discovery, Dr.

Shettles set out to find some means of exploiting this new knowledge to help parents choose the sex of their children. Since there definitely seemed to be a difference in the overall size of the two types of sperm, he reasoned that there must be other differences as well. Perhaps one type was stronger than the other or faster —or both. Perhaps one type could survive longer in a certain environment than the other. There were all sorts of intriguing possibilities that could lead to a means of selecting sex—simply by interfering, even slightly, with the environment in which the sperm seeks out the egg.

It seems quite probable that the larger, female-producing sperm (now called gynosperm) must be more resistant than the other type. Why should there be nearly twice as many of the smaller, boy-producing variety (known as androsperm) in the ejaculate of the average male if not to compensate for some inferiority in coping with the environment beyond the male reproductive tract? There may be as many as 170 boys conceived for every 100 girls, and for every 100 female births, there are about 105 male births. In terms of longevity, resistance to disease and stress and adaptability to environment, it has long been conceded, at least by scientists, that the male is the weaker of the two sexes. This fact now appears to be borne out even at the most elemental level; the male-producing sperm begin with a substantial head start (perhaps a 2–1 margin) but end up only slightly ahead of the female-producing sperm in the number of babies born each year.

What accounts for the greater slaughter of androsperm within the womb? To find out, Dr. Shettles began studying the environment that exists inside the vagina and uterus at about the time of conception. He took transparent capillary tubes and filled them with cervical and vaginal secretions. Then he turned millions of sperm loose at the opening of the tubes and watched their activity through his microscope.

"It was a little like watching the races at Belmont," he said. When the secretions in the tubes were more acidic than alkaline, the gynosperm seemed to prevail. But when the tubes were filled with cervical mucus removed from a woman very close to the time of ovulation, the smaller androsperm were clear-cut winners nearly every time. Why?

Acid inhibits both gynosperm and androsperm, but it harms the androsperm first and most, cutting them out of the herd and thus out of competition. The gynosperm's greater bulk seems to protect them from the acid for much longer periods than their little brothers are able to survive.

Alkaline secretions are kind to both types of sperm and generally enhance the chances for fertilization. But in the absence of hostile acids, the androsperm are able to use the *one* advantage they have over their sisters: the speed and the agility that their small, compact heads and long tails give them.

As a gynecologist, Dr. Shettles knew that the environment within the vagina is generally acidic, while the environment within the cervix and uterus is generally alkaline. And he knew that the closer a woman gets to ovulation the more alkaline her cervical secretions become. All of this told him that *timing of intercourse* is a critical factor in choosing the sex of children. His findings suggested that intercourse at or very close to the time of ovulation, when the secretions are most alkaline, would very likely result in male offspring. Intercourse two or three days before the time of ovulation, on the other hand, when an acid environment still prevails, would be likely to yield female offspring. The female-producing sperm cells can survive those two or three days, while the androsperm rarely last longer than twenty-four hours.

Certain now that he was on the right track, Dr. Shettles began looking through the scientific and historic literature for further confirmation. He found that Orthodox Jews produce significantly more male offspring than does the general population, and he began consulting rabbis and poring over the Talmud, a compilation of Jewish beliefs and laws. One of the passages he found was this: "The determination of sex takes place at the moment of cohabitation. When the woman emits semen before the man [meaning when she experiences orgasm before her husband], the child will be a boy. Otherwise it will be a girl." If a boy were desired, the Talmud directed the husband to "hold back" until his wife experienced orgasm. Dr. Shettles found another clue in Orthodox Jewish law: Women must not engage in intercourse during their "unclean" period (menstruation) or for one week thereafter.

Both of these directives coincided very neatly with Dr. Shettles' findings. Orgasm is the less important of the two factors, but it can play a part in sex selection. Female orgasm helps provide additional alkaline secretions. Of course, many women (perhaps 40 per cent) never experience orgasm. These women should not think that their chances to conceive boys are diminished, because there are other ways of increasing the alkalinity that favors male offspring. The other point—abstaining from intercourse until at least a week after the conclusion of menstruation—is more significant, for this puts coitus very close to the time of ovulation in most women.

Dr. Shettles also sifted through the data on artificial insemination. Doctors specializing in artificial insemination report that they try to pinpoint the time of ovulation in their patients so that fertilization can be achieved on the first try. It occurred to Dr. Shettles that an unintended side effect of this practice ought to be an abundance of male offspring. In a series of several thousand births achieved by artificial insemination, he found that the sex ratio was 160 males for every 100 females. In another series, 76 per cent were boys and 24 per cent were girls!

Elated that his hunch seemed to be correct, Dr. Shettles began startling some of his patients by telling them that they no longer had to rely on the whims of Mother Nature—at least not entirely—when it came to the sex of their children.

Another of Dr. Shettles' findings in the course of his early research was that low sperm count seems to be associated with a preponderance of female offspring. Men with high sperm count, on the other hand, tend to father a greater number of male offspring. This suggested that building up the sperm count through abstinence from intercourse might be another way of increasing chances for male offspring.

As a result of these findings, Dr. Shettles has formulated two procedures—one to be used if a female child is desired, the other if a male is wanted. These procedures can be used in the home *without* prior semen analysis.

*The procedure for female offspring:*

1. Intercourse should cease two or three days before ovulation. Timing is the most important factor.

2. Intercourse should be immediately *preceded,* on each occasion, by an acidic douche consisting of two tablespoons of *white* vinegar to a quart of water. The timing might be enough to ensure female offspring, but the douche makes success all the more likely, since the acid environment immobilizes the androsperm.

3. If the wife normally has orgasm, she should try to avoid it. Orgasm increases the flow of alkaline secretions, and these could neutralize or weaken the acid environment that enhances the chances of the gynosperm.

4. The face-to-face, or "missionary," position should be assumed during intercourse. Dr. Shettles believes that this makes it less likely that sperm will be deposited directly at the mouth of the cervix, where they might escape the acid environment of the vagina.

5. Shallow penetration by the male at the time of male orgasm is recommended. Again, this helps make certain that the sperm are exposed to the acid in the vagina and must swim through it to get to the cervix.

6. No abstinence from intercourse is necessary, until after the final intercourse two or three days before ovulation. A low sperm count increases the possibility of female offspring, so frequent intercourse, prior to

the final try two or three days before ovulation, cannot hurt and may actually help. This may be why Dr. Shettles says "having girls is more fun."

*The procedure for male offspring:*

1. Intercourse should be timed as close to the moment of ovulation as possible.

2. Intercourse should be immediately preceded, on each occasion, by a baking-soda douche, consisting of two tablespoons of baking soda to a quart of water. The solution should be permitted to stand for fifteen minutes before use. This allows the soda to become completely dissolved.

3. Female orgasm is not necessary but is desirable. If a woman normally has orgasm, her husband should time his to coincide with hers or let her experience orgasm first.

4. Vaginal penetration from the rear is the recommended position. This, Dr. Shettles says, helps ensure deposition of sperm at the entrance of the womb. This is desirable because the secretions within the cervix and womb will be highly alkaline, more so even than in the vagina in spite of the alkaline douches, and an alkaline environment is most favorable to androsperm.

5. Deep penetration at the moment of male orgasm will help ensure deposition of sperm close to the cervix.

6. Prior abstinence is *necessary;* intercourse should be avoided completely from the beginning of the monthly cycle until the day of ovulation. This helps ensure maximum sperm count, a factor favoring androsperm.

"All of this means," Dr. Shettles observes, "that if the first intercourse of the cycle takes place right at ovulation time, the male sperm will race along like a cab going through Broadway on a green light." If, however, intercourse takes place two or three days before ovulation, most of the male sperm will be incapacitated by the time the egg arrives. "For the female sperm," Dr. Shettles continues, "it's like flying into LaGuardia on a foggy night. They have to hover around and wait for the signal. Then they zoom right in."

Dr. Shettles does not guarantee that these procedures will be successful on *every* occasion. But he says, "The procedures are safe and simple. There's nothing distasteful about them, nothing any religious body has objected to. They can be carried out in the home and they are entirely harmless. Clinical results show at least 80 per cent success. And I believe that if the couple is conscientious with the douche and the timing, they can achieve success 85 to 90 per cent of the time."

Dr. Shettles reports that all babies born after use of these techniques have been completely normal. Neither douche is harmful to mother or offspring. The safest applicator for either douche is the hot-water-bottle type. Let the fluid flow under the force of gravity alone. It is not harmful to use the douches repeatedly before each intercourse during the fertile period. Remember, though, that douching should be used in conjunction with timing of intercourse and may not by itself be sufficient to tip the balance in the desired direction.

Pinpointing the time of ovulation is of vital importance. Most women ovulate between days eleven and fifteen of the average menstrual cycle, but each woman must determine her own ovulation time. Generally, women are told to keep a temperature chart. Your doctor is familiar with this procedure and can instruct you in it, if necessary. This procedure involves a special but inexpensive thermometer scored in tenths of a degree so that even tiny variations aren't missed. Temperature is taken orally each day before getting out of bed in the morning and then is recorded on the chart. Typically, temperature will remain about even throughout menstruation and will probably rise or fall two- or three-tenths of a degree over the next several days. A sudden dip of perhaps two-tenths of a degree or more in temperature over a period of a single day indicates that ovulation is at hand, though no one is certain whether ovulation takes place at the bottom of the dip or as it begins to rise again. The temperature will rise sharply again, usually within a day, and remain high, indicating that ovulation has taken place.

Women should maintain records for two or, preferably, three or four months before using them for sex selection. And women who have been on the birth-control pill, Dr. Shettles says, should wait four to six months after discontinuing use of The Pill before attempting to select sex. These months can be used to determine the exact time of ovulation.

The temperature approach has proved far from ideal for many women. For one thing, if the woman is emotionally upset, ill, or if she smokes, eats or moves about before taking her temperature each morning, the charts are not likely to be very accurate. Because of the instability of the temperature approach and the difficulties of interpretation, Dr. Shettles recommends a newer and more accurate procedure. This involves the purchase of a fertility test kit (available at most drugstores without prescription for about $7) or for less money, but equally good, a little roll of Tes-Tape, also available at most drugstores without prescription. Tes-Tape is a roll of special yellow paper that comes in a Scotch Tape-type dispenser; the tape turns varying shades of blue and green when exposed to glucose, which is abundant in cervical mucus at the time of ovulation.

Beginning at the end of menstruation, start off each day, Dr. Shettles instructs, by tearing off a three-inch strip of tape. Bend the strip over the index finger and secure it with a small rubber band. Now guide the finger into the vagina so that the tip of your finger and the tape make contact with the cervix, which will feel something like the tip of your nose. Hold the finger gently up against the cervix for ten to fifteen seconds, then withdraw it. Note the color of the tape at the tip of your finger. Early in the cycle it probably won't change color at all. Or it might change to a light green. As you approach ovulation, each new tape will be darker and darker. Consult the color chart on the Tes-Tape or fertility kit dispenser. When the color of the tape matches the darkest color on the scale (a deep greenish blue), you will know that ovulation is at hand. (Note that the Tes-Tape chart is coded for the urine test—used by diabetics—but it works for ovulation as well.)

Dr. Shettles recommends that you experiment with the procedure through three or four cycles before using it for the critical intercourse. In this way, you can determine the day on which you normally ovulate and what color the tape is two and three days before it turns its darkest hue. This latter information will be important if you are trying for a girl. Keep careful records of the approximate color that turns up each day. Five different color bars are indicated on the Tes-Tape chart, so you may want to number these one through five, starting with yellow, and jot down the applicable number each day.

Test the cervical mucus two or three times a day as it approaches its darkest hue, so that if a boy is wanted, you can time coitus as closely as possible to ovulation. Always use the Tes-Tape before intercourse and, of course, before either of the two douches. If you are using the Tes-Tape or fertility kit (which comes equipped with an applicator) incorrectly, consult your doctor.

The further away from ovulation that one times intercourse, the more difficult it is to achieve pregnancy. But it is also true that when one does achieve pregnancy in these cases, the offspring is very likely to be female. If a couple wants a girl, it is wise to time intercourse three days prior to ovulation, Dr. Shettles says. If after three or four months, they have still not achieved pregnancy on this schedule, they should move to a two-and-a-half-day interval. At two days it is still far more likely that female offspring will result (provided the other procedures are also followed). But the couple wanting a girl has nothing to lose by starting out with the more cautious three-day interval. Pregnancy can and does occur in a significant number of cases under these circumstances. If intercourse takes place up to seven hours *after* ovulation, a boy will be the most likely result. Cervical secretions are still quite abundant and highly alkaline during this period, but Dr. Shettles suggests testing the secretions to be sure.

The clinical results of these timing procedures are encouraging. "With exposure to pregnancy two to twenty-four hours before ovulation," Dr. Sophia Kleegman (a gynecologist Dr. Shettles has been working with) reports, "the babies were predominantly male (78 per cent). With exposure to pregnancy thirty-six or more hours before ovulation, the babies were predominantly female."

In another study, Dr. Shettles reported that one group of twenty-two couples who wanted female offspring took up to six months to conceive by timing intercourse two to three days before ovulation. "Of twenty-two offspring," he notes, "nineteen were girls (86 per cent). In a group of twenty-six women anxious to have boys, the first coitus occurred at the time of ovulation or within twelve hours thereafter. To these women, twenty-three boys were born (88 per cent)."

Elsewhere, other researchers are trying to bring this already impressive average up to 100 per cent, primarily by attempting to separate the two types of sperm. Early experiments along these lines—using animal sperm—yielded only partial success. One approach to separating the two types of sperm—called "electrophoresis"—is based on the assumption that the two types have different electrical charges and thus might be polarized by electric current. Dr. Manuel Gordon of Michigan State University has enjoyed some success with this approach, though far from the 100 percent hoped for. Dr. Gordon placed rabbit sperm in a saline solution and then passed electrical current through it. The male-producing sperm tended to migrate toward the negative electrical pole while the female type headed for the positive pole. Inseminating rabbits with cells from the negative pole, Dr. Gordon produced males 64 per cent of the time; with sperm from the positive pole he got females 71 per cent of the time. These results are encouraging enough so that electrophoresis is not very likely to be abandoned without further work.

Another approach is centrifugation, a technique that exploits the difference in mass between the two types of sperm. The centrifuge is an instrument that spins the sperm around and around until the two types become stratified, each type falling into its own zone according to mass, with the heavier (female) on the bottom and the lighter (male) on the top. Swedish scientists have had considerable success with this, achieving in their initial study the births of eleven male calves in a row by using sperm of lesser mass. Others have had less satisfactory results, accountable, perhaps, by a difference in centrifugation technique.

Very good results have been obtained by using yet a third method of separation: sedimentation. The earliest work in this field was done by Dr. B. C. Bhattacharya, an Indian zoologist, who noticed that peasants in his country preferred to bring their cows in for artificial insemination at sundown rather than earlier in the day, claiming that this resulted in more male offspring. Dr. Bhattacharya, skeptical at first, checked into this and found that it was true! Cattle inseminated later in the day *did* produce more male calves. Looking for a scientific explanation, he concluded that the two types of sperm drifted to the bottom of storage containers at different rates, the heavier female-producing variety reaching the bottom first. By the end of the day, he reasoned, far more of the lighter, male-producing sperm would be left at the top of the containers, which would explain why more bull calves were conceived at sundown.

At the famed Max Planck Institute for Animal Breeding (at Hagen, Germany), Dr. Bhattacharya undertook a series of experiments, inseminating thousands of rabbits with sperm that had settled under a variety of conditions. He finally found that the best results could be obtained by refrigerating the sperm (mixed in a protective solution of egg yolk and glycerol) for about twelve hours at just above freezing. This prevented the sperm from swimming about, and in their immobile state they separated far better than they had previously. Dr. Bhattacharya used the refrigerated samples to impregnate 176 rabbits. Sperm from the bottom of the containers produced 72 per cent females. Sperm from the top yielded males 78 per cent of the time.

Encouraged by this, Dr. Bhattacharya is hopeful that the technique can be refined to the point where the two types of sperm can be completely segregated. It will probably be some time, however, before Dr. Bhattacharya's batting average surpasses that already achieved by Dr. Shettles and Dr. Kleegman.

One of the most exciting future prospects is envisioned by Dr. E. James Leiberman of the National Institutes of Health in Washington, D.C. Dr. Leiberman foresees the day when women will have at their disposal "special diaphragms that will let through only the sperm that carries, let's say, the male sex and hold back those that carry the female sex." Selecting sex, then, would simply become a matter of which diaphragm one chooses to wear. Dr. Charles Birch, head of the Sydney (Australia) University School of Biological Sciences, goes even further, predicting that science will one day come up with a pill to determine sex. When males are desired, Prof. Birch says the husband will simply take one of the "little-boy pills" just before intercourse or, if a female is wanted, one of the "little-girl pills." When one stops to think how effective even such commonplace chemicals as vinegar and baking soda can be, Dr. Birch's idea doesn't really seem all that utopian, after all. Nor does it seem unreasonable to expect that such pills—probably coming in shades of pink and blue—will become available within the next two or, at most, three decades.

Even in the event that all of these methods fail to achieve the desired sex every time, there is yet another approach to sex selection that leaves open no opportunity whatever for failure. It is far more controversial than the techniques discussed so far, for reasons that will become apparent. Cambridge University physiologists Richard Gardner and Robert Edwards mated rabbits, then removed the embryos before they had attached themselves to the linings of their mothers' wombs. Then, using microsurgical tools, they removed a few hundred cells from each embryo and examined them under the microscope for the presence of sex chromatin, found only in female cells. In this way they were able to separate the tiny embryos into males and females at the very earliest stages of their development!

After letting the embryos recover from microsurgery—by bathing them in culture mediums for several hours—the scientists implanted them in slits that were made in the wombs of the mother rabbits. The embryos then developed naturally and in every case turned out at birth to be the sex that the researchers had predicted.

Of course, if a woman wanted to control the sex of her offspring in this way, she would have to have in many cases more than one embryo to choose from at the beginning. This is possible since there are drugs, discussed in the preceding chapter, that can induce "superovulation," or the release of many eggs at once —instead of the normal one per month. Then, when all of these are fertilized, but before they attach themselves to the lining of the uterus, they could be washed out of the fallopian tubes and "sexed" under the microscope. That is, they could be separated into males and females, in the same fashion that the rabbit embryos were. Then, if a boy is desired, one of the males could be implanted in the uterus and the rest of the embryos discarded.

It is this discarding that invites controversy. The British journal *New Scientist* has expressed doubt about the moral and ethical aspects of the procedure: "Dr. Edwards' plan takes no account of those 'bench' embryos not selected for survival. Would their destruction by the laboratory attendant who cleaned up after a day's work amount to an act of abortion?" That depends, of course, upon the point at which society says life begins. Currently, the Catholic Church maintains that life commences at the moment of conception, when sperm and egg merge in the fallopian tube. There is some chance, however, that this definition may be modified, since a number of prominent scientists, such as Dr. A. S. Parkes, believe that nidation— the point at which the embryo attaches itself to the lining of the womb—should mark the real beginning of life, since it is only at this point that the embryo really begins to develop or has any chance of developing. If this view ultimately prevails, there can be no objections to the Edwards approach—an approach that guarantees the sex you want every time.

For the time being there seems to be no religious problem associated with the Shettles method of sex selection. Protestant ministers have inquired about the procedures with the intention of incorporating them into their own family planning programs, rabbis have cooperated with Dr. Shettles in his research and the Roman Catholic Church has bestowed its blessing. Msgr. Hugh Curran, director of the Family Life Bureau of the Archdiocese of New York, says that the Church has no objections to Dr. Shettles' sex-selection procedures "as long as the intent of these efforts is not to prevent conception."

There have been objections—other than religious— raised in connection with sex selection. Dr. Amitai Etzioni, a professor of sociology at Columbia University, for example, fears that sex-selection techniques will give rise to a bumper crop of boys, with various unpleasant consequences, including a rise in the incidence of homosexuality. Others point out that if girls should become the rage society would have to give its blessings to polygamy; if boys should become the vogue then polyandry would have to prevail. "The dangers are not apocalyptic," Prof. Etzioni concedes, "but are they worth the gains to be made?"

It seems likely that most prospective parents would answer with a "yes." And though only time will tell the story, Dr. Shettles is convinced that parents will not use his techniques—or others under development —to produce males at the expense of females, or vice versa. He points out that a temporary overabundance of one sex will automatically result in a big demand for the other sex and notes that "over the years, parents have expressed only one desire and that is to have families that are well balanced in terms of sex. Most find an equal number of boys and girls ideal."

Dr. Paul Ehrlich, the prominent Stanford University population biologist, has repeatedly called for stepped-up research in the field of sex selection, stating that many couples would limit their families to two children if they could achieve the ideal one-boy/one-girl balance on their first two tries. Dr. Shettles is of the same opinion, noting that dozens of couples have told him that they initially planned for families of two children, hoping for one of each sex. But when both offspring turned out to be of the same sex, they made a third attempt and so on. Hence it is not at all farfetched to envision sex selection, given all-out encouragement by society, making a significant contribution to the effort to control the ever more destructive population explosion. The advantages of sex selection are manifest: parental satisfaction, balanced families, smaller families and, very possibly, *healthier* families.

Sometimes health—or lack of it—is attached to our sex chromosomes. Only males, for example, suffer from hemophilia, the grim and often fatal "bleeder's disease." Similar hereditary, sex-linked diseases include one type of muscular dystrophy and numerous enzyme-deficiency disorders that can kill, cripple and retard for life. The value of sex selection in helping overcome these diseases motivates many researchers in the field, such as Drs. Edwards and Gardner at Cambridge. Writing in *New Scientist*, they point out

that "the elimination of these disorders in one generation, by a judicious choice of the sex of the offspring,
would not only be of direct benefit to that generation,
but would benefit the race for generations to come."

There are still other advantages that could accrue
from our ability to choose the sex of our children. Dr.
A. L. Benedict has suggested that sex selection might
have some psychological benefits—beyond those that
accrue from sexually balanced families. Some parents,
Dr. Benedict believes, are really only suited to raise
children of one sex. It may be that a woman who has
a strong aversion for little girls is mentally disturbed
and shouldn't really have *any* children. But since she
is likely to go ahead no matter what her neighbors
think, isn't it better if she has nothing but boys—better
for her offspring as well as for herself? Similarly, there
are men who have such a strong desire to beget children of one sex that their offspring, should they turn
out to be of the "wrong" gender, suffer for it. The
father's disappointment is quickly communicated to
the child, very often without words, and the child
may, as many a psychiatric case history has shown,
feel at once rejected and guilty—guilty for having
"failed" to be born a member of the opposite sex. The
child may then either withdraw into himself or perhaps
try to "correct" his error by acting as though he were
indeed a member of the opposite sex. If the situation
continues to deteriorate, the child could be psychologically scarred for life, unable to function properly in his
biologically assigned sexual role.

All in all, sex selection appears to be a product of
the Biological Revolution fraught with more promise
than peril. Still, the fears of such men as Prof. Etzioni
cannot be completely discounted. Certainly it would
seem wise that some agency of society should, as a
minimum precaution, explore means of heading off
factors that might fuel boy-girl fads and develop plans
for dealing with such situations if they should occur
anyway.

# FOUR

# Fetal Surgery: Operating on the Unborn

The woman on the operating table was incredibly determined. At thirty-one, she had already suffered eight miscarriages. Now, about seven months pregnant, her stomach was swollen with a ninth effort to bring a child into the world alive. "I want this baby," she had cried a few hours before, knowing that the life within her was in grave peril, that its sole chance was a breathtaking surgical procedure attempted only a few times before and never with any success. "I don't care if it's deformed," she had said. "Even if you have to cut off a leg I still want it." Under the effects of the drug Halothane, administered at several times its usual dosage, she appeared near death. Only the eerie blips on the life-function monitoring screens reassured the assembled doctors that the woman and—equally important—the patient within her womb were still alive.

One of the attending fetologists made a six-inch incision from the navel to an area over the urinary bladder, exposing a sizable portion of the uterus. Having thus initiated his first attempt at fetal surgery, he consulted X-ray plates and then deftly penetrated the uterine wall, making a one-and-a-half-inch opening. Through this small aperture the doctors peered down onto the amniotic sac, a paper-thin capsule designed by nature to sustain the fetus during its nine-month odyssey through inner space, a "journey" immeasurably more complex, perilous and wondrous than those endured by our moon-bound astronauts.

The capsule was snipped open, and one of the doctors dipped into the waters of the capsule with forceps and fished up a fetal leg just a few inches long and so delicate that it could only be held with hands in fluid-filled gloves. While an assistant bathed the unborn leg in a warm saline solution, one of the fetologists sought out an area near the groin, directly over the saphenous vein that carries blood back to the heart. Here he made another incision, implanted a catheter into the vein and tied it into place. Through this tiny lifeline, the surgical team removed most of the baby's blood— the vital red cells which had been ravaged by marauding antibodies from the mother's blood stream—and replaced it with new blood rich in these cells. Three hours later, the catheter was removed, the incision in the groin was closed and the leg was gently eased back into its underwater refuge.

"We didn't go home after that operation," recalls Dr. Stanley Asensio, one of the fetologists and an associate professor of obstetrics and gynecology at the University of Puerto Rico Medical School. "We slept right there with the patient for days, afraid something might go wrong." The only previous attempts at human fetal surgery, at Columbia-Presbyterian Medical Center in New York, had resulted in premature labor and delivery, in some cases shortly after surgery. "The uterus is a highly reactive organ," Dr. Asensio explains. "Once it is entered, some unknown mechanism generally starts it contracting, and the fetus is pushed out." When labor did not develop during the first forty-eight-hour period, Dr. Asensio and the other doctors concluded that the Halothane—which prevents the uterus from contracting—and careful surgical management had done their jobs.

"Essentially what we were trying to do with this operation," Dr. Asensio says, "was to buy time. The fetus was so anemic on account of Rh disease that it would have died *in utero*, almost immediately, if we hadn't operated." The Rh factor, named after the rhesus monkeys in which it was first isolated, is present in the blood of 85 per cent of the population. When it is present, the blood is Rh positive; when it is absent, Rh negative. When an Rh-negative woman bears an Rh-positive baby (as a result of mating with an Rh-positive male), her body may become sensitized and develop antibodies to fend off the "foreign" invaders. This is by no means rare. Some 10 per cent of all Caucasian marriages are incompatible from the Rh point of view—a formidable number. (The incidence is somewhat lower for other races.) Thousands of babies die each year in the womb because of this disease, technically known as *erythroblastosis fetalis*. "We were hoping to keep the fetus alive for another month," Dr. Asensio explains. "Then we thought it would be big and strong enough to withstand premature delivery [at eight months] and undergo further transfusions outside the womb."

But three weeks after that historic operation, the woman, now almost eight months pregnant, began passing amniotic fluid through the cervix, an indication either that she was about to go into labor or that membranes were broken and that she was susceptible to infection. "We agonized over what to do," Dr. Asensio recalls. "If she wasn't going into labor and we waited that extra week, we might get a baby not dead of anemia but of infection. So we called a meeting. It looked like the legislature had convened. We agreed to terminate the pregnancy at once."

A Cesarean section yielded a baby girl, one month premature and still anemic—though not nearly so anemic as she had been three weeks before. Today, four years later, the baby is healthy and normal in every respect. Only now does Dr. Asensio feel that he can call the operation a major medical breakthrough.

Since that first operation, the Puerto Rico team has

performed even bolder surgical forays into the world of the unborn. They operated on one twenty-week-old fetus that weighed little more than a pound, removed another entirely from the uterus for more than a half hour before returning it to the womb with a catheter implanted in its jugular vein. Though the Rh problem now generally yields to less radical treatment, the open-surgical technique that Dr. Asensio employed is expected to intervene in a variety of problems that previously killed or crippled thousands of babies, or left them mentally retarded.

Fetal surgery is the most dazzling property of a dramatic new medical subspecialty known as fetology. As medicine's newest science, it is devoted to medicine's newest—and youngest—patient, the fetus. Dr. Sheldon Cherry, a pioneering fetologist at Mount Sinai Hospital in New York, says fetology "has humanized the fetus." Until recently, Dr. Cherry notes, the fetus was regarded by the bewildered mother, the obstetrician and the pediatrician as a quasi-living thing. "Let nature take her course and keep your hands off was the general rule," Dr. Asensio says. "Until a few years ago, the fetus was absolutely taboo, a mystery, an untouchable."

Only in the last decade have doctors come to regard this attitude as something mounting very nearly to criminal negligence. There are some 65,000 stillbirths in this country each year; another 67,000 babies, damaged during pregnancy and labor, fail to survive the first four weeks. (This is three times the number of children who die from all causes between the ages of one and fourteen each year.) In addition, a quarter-million babies are born brain-damaged annually. Facing these facts, obstetricians and pediatricians are gradually uniting to cope with the problems of the fetus, attempting to provide continuum care from earliest pregnancy through birth.

More than anything else, Rh disease has provided fetology with the challenge that it needed to grow and expand. In the early 1950s, a British doctor named

D. C. A. Bevis, ignoring the centuries-old taboo, injected a long needle through the abdomen of a pregnant woman and drew out a few drops of amber-colored amniotic fluid. Analysis of the bilirubin (a pigment of red blood cells) in the syringe enabled Dr. Bevis to tell just how sick the fetus was. Doctors began using this technique, known as amniocentesis, to tell them when they ought to induce labor prematurely so that the fetus could undergo immediate post-natal transfusion. This cut the death rate from Rh disease in many hospitals by more than 50 per cent.

Yet thousands of babies continued to die, since induced birth before seven months cannot generally succeed—and even at seven months it is perilous. Rh disease can threaten life as early as four months. The answer to this dilemma came in 1963 when Dr. A. William Liley of New Zealand accidentally pierced a fetal abdomen during aminiocentesis. Since the fetus seemed none the worse for the experience, apart from the detectable start it gave (Dr. Liley could feel it jump), he decided to use the technique to feed new blood into the fetus. Fetuses proved to have the unique ability to absorb red blood cells that were injected directly into their abdomens. This has further reduced deaths from Rh disease, so that at some hospitals mortality now runs at only 3 or 4 per cent where it used to be in the neighborhood of 30 per cent.

To help them hit their tiny targets, doctors developed a number of new procedures. Dr. Cherry developed a metal grill which, when placed over the abdomens of his pregnant patients during X raying, provides multiple reference points for positioning of the needle.

Dr. John T. Queenan injects an X-ray absorbent dye into the amniotic fluid that the fetus swallows. The dye lights up the tiny gastrointestinal tract on a fluoroscopic screen and thus gives the fetologist a clearly defined target. Then Dr. Queenan introduces a tracer needle that emits a visible trail of its own by releasing small jets of similar radiopaque material. He guides the needle to the lighted abdominal cavity—watching his progress on a television-like screen.

Dr. Maclyn Wade of Yale has used yet a different technique—one involving a fiber-optic amnioscope, a viewing device that permits one to look right inside the womb without potentially dangerous X rays and fluoroscopy. This device channels light to the site under investigation through tiny hollow fibers whose heatless tips glow like Fourth of July sparklers. The fetologist inserts the needle-like instrument into the amniotic sac, entering through the abdomen, and views the contents from outside. A tiny transparent balloon on the end of the device pushes the murky fluid aside and acts as a sort of underwater mask for better viewing. In one instance, Dr. Wade used the technique to transfuse a single fetus five times.

Other researchers, led by Dr. Vincent J. Freda of the Columbia-Presbyterian Medical Center, set out to prevent the Rh problem from ever developing in the mother. They created a serum called RhoGam, which is administered to the Rh-negative mother *after* rather than before each birth, since the baby's Rh-positive blood seeps into the mother's system through the placenta during delivery, thereby signaling the manufacture of antibodies. This is why the woman usually has her first baby with little or no difficulty. But by the time her second and third babies come along, her antibodies have built up and are lying in wait. RhoGam, which is effective only for women not already sensitized, tricks the mother's immune system by temporarily populating her blood with Rh antibodies, thus preventing it from producing its own permanent, deadly antibodies.

At first glance, this major medical coup would seem to render any further fetology work unnecessary. But the procedures that were developed in the fight against Rh disease are, in the words of one fetologist, "going on to bigger and better things, finding new applications every day." Fiberoptic amnioscopy, for example, is presently being developed by German researchers to the point where it can be used to direct minor surgery without opening the womb. "There are amnioscopes in experimental use," Dr. Asensio notes, "through which you can view the fetus and introduce tiny knives to take fetal blood and skin samples and even perform certain surgical procedures, cutting with the blade and cauterizing with electric current." Most authorities agree that amnioscopy and fetal surgery are only in their infancy, that they will have applications that reach far beyond treatment of fetal anemia.

As new tools and techniques have become available, fetal surgery has made giant strides. To date, Dr. Asensio and team have performed five open operations and have had three successes. The problem that has plagued fetal surgeons at Yale, Columbia and elsewhere—premature labor—complicated one of Dr. Asensio's cases, in spite of heavy doses of Halothane. So Dr. Asensio resorted to a still controversial technique pioneered by Dr. Fritz Fuchs at Cornell University Medical Center. A few hours after surgery the patient, carrying a thirty-week-old fetus, went into labor.

"This was a small baby," Dr. Asensio observes, "and I knew we needed another few weeks before we could safely deliver. Fuchs had done experiments to forestall labor by injecting alcohol into the blood of his patients. Though the circumstances were somewhat different here—the labor had been induced by surgery—we decided to try it out." So for ten days a woman lay in a San Juan hospital, "completely drunk, singing, happy and free of pain."

More important, she was free of labor contractions —until the eleventh day, when she failed to get her "booster" of 20 per cent alcohol on time. In spite of this, the baby was delivered sober but in high spirits, and the mother proved to be unharmed by her eleven-day binge. Further testing is necessary, but, as one doctor put it, "booze could conceivably knock out the biggest fetal killer of all—prematurity."

Though many surgical attempts have ended in failure, this is nothing to be alarmed at, says Dr. Ronald E. Myers, chief of the National Institute of Health Laboratory of Perinatal Physiology in San Juan. "After all," he notes, "most of the doctors have had only a handful of patients so far. Look how long it took open-heart surgery to begin yielding good results."

As a neurologist, Dr. Myers is concerned with the prenatal circumstances that cause such common defects as mental retardation and cerebral palsy. Experimenting with animals (primarily monkeys), he interferes surgically with the vascular and respiratory processes of the fetus and observes the results after bringing it to term. In this way he is able to begin uncovering the causes of many diseases and defects. And in the course of his experimentation, he says, "we found that success or failure in fetal surgery is dependent on the maintenance of normal respiration in the mother. There is a paradox her in the sense that the well-intentioned physician is generally inclined to give the mother a lot of oxygen." Dr. Myers initially believed that himself, thinking that added oxygen might "optimize fetal survival." Instead, it caused irritation of the uterine musculature and consequent expulsion of the fetus.

"With more experience," Dr. Myers is confident, "the human fetologists will be able to look forward to a survival rate of at least 60 per cent." Fetologists at Columbia, Yale and the University of Puerto Rico hope to tackle certain heart-and-vessel defects, diaphragmatic hernias that lead to malformation of the lungs, fetal tumors, hearing defects, superfetation (the presence of so many fetuses in the womb, as a result of taking fertility drugs, that none can survive) and hydrocephalus, a disease in which fluid concentrates in the head and damages the brain. The latter is a particularly big killer and one that some doctors think can be virtually eliminated with fetal surgery. The procedure for treating it will be relatively simple. Doctors will open the womb, remove the fetus, or at least its head, from the womb and implant a shunt between scalp and skull to drain off the fluid that otherwise crushes the brain. The shunt will be so arranged that it will drain into the amniotic fluid rather than to some point outside the mother's body, thus minimizing chances for outside infection.

Ultimately, fetal surgeons expect to attempt fetal transplants. Because the fetus does not yet have a functioning immunological system (the system that operates in the well-known rejection syndrome so common to heart transplants among adults), it will readily accept tissue grafts. As Dr. Myers notes, "If you go to the early fetus, it is pretty fantastic what you can do—like take the arm off one animal and put it on another, change sex or even transplant heads." Needless to say, Dr. Myers does not necessarily endorse such radical procedures; he simply points out that they are possible.

Preventive medicine and early diagnosis of ailments have always been the best way to avoid surgery. This is true in fetology as it is in every other branch of medicine. Hence, even as fetal surgeons have been perfecting spectacular techniques, other doctors have been just as busy developing procedures to help make surgery unnecessary. Apart from the RhoGam vaccine, for example, doctors have recently marketed another serum—this one for the prevention of German measles. It was known for some time that viruses could inflict grotesque damage on the unborn, but it was not until 1965—"Year of the Bitter Harvest"—that a preventive crash program was initiated. It was in 1965 that thousands of children were born blind, deaf and brain-damaged due to the fact that their mothers had picked up the rubella (German measles) virus during pregnancy. Now there is a vaccine to prevent such tragedies in the future.

It is becoming increasingly apparent that the fetus is not an isolated organism, shut off from its mother and the outside world. It is both receptive and vulnerable to chemicals that enter the mother, either by design or by chance. This fact was brought home—tragically—to medical scientists a few years ago when it became apparent that some of the chemical constituents of Thalidomide, a tranquilizer, had crossed the supposedly impermeable placental barrier that separates mother and fetus. The result was that millions of unborn babies were severely deformed.

Drugs can help as well as harm, of course, and doctors are now coming to the realization that one need not wait for birth before writing out prescriptions for their patients. Dr. Robert E. Cooke, pediatrician in chief at Johns Hopkins Hospital and an associate of one of the nation's first major centers to detect inherited defects before birth, believes that there are a number of defects that can be treated while the fetus is still in the womb, among them cystic fibrosis and various enzyme diseases. Typical of the latter is Tay-Sachs disease, a hereditary illness that is almost invariably fatal to the fetus. A missing enzyme is the sole cause of this disease, according to recent findings at the University of California, and Dr. John S. O'Brien and Dr. Shintaro Okado are presently at work trying to eliminate the disease by introducing the missing enzyme into the womb.

Dr. Virginia Apgar, developer of the well-known Apgar scale that is used to determine the health of newborns, is another doctor interested in implementing a wide-scale program of preventive medicine for the unborn. She points out that it is far easier to get the fetus to take its medicine than it is to persuade most children to do the same. "The fetus swallows the amniotic fluid continually," she observes, "and so would readily ingest whatever drug we might choose to introduce."

Dr. Apgar and associates are establishing a pilot program in New York aimed at detecting fetal ills and treating them before it is too late. "When blood is drawn for pre-marital venereal disease tests, the samples will also be tested for German measles antibodies and for the Rh factor," she says. "If a woman is not immune to German measles, she then could receive the vaccine to protect her future children. If she and her husband may produce a baby with Rh disease, she could take the RhoGam vaccine to prevent that problem."

Other diseases such as toxoplasma gondii, a crippling parasite, Dr. Apgar believes, could easily be treated before birth by injecting into the amnion the proper drugs. The parasites are frequently ingested in undercooked meat and raw eggs. They cause little trouble in adults but can be fatal to the fetus, inflicting on them a number of defects, including hydrocephalus.

In order to treat these various ills, of course, one must first detect them. Fortunately, new systems and procedures are developing almost daily for the detection of fetal diseases and the monitoring of fetal health. Ultrasound, for example, is now being used, without any of the dangers of X rays, to visualize the fetus. Doctors at some centers are now routinely bouncing pulses of ultrasound off their unborn patients—right through the abdominal walls of their mothers—quickly, painlessly, harmlessly. These pulses and the pattern in which they are reflected or deflected are translated by a computer-like machine into dots that trace on paper an outline of the baby's body. In this way doctors are able to determine such things as the shape of the skull and hence such defects as hydrocephalus (the "water-on-the-brain" disease, characterized by a large swollen head) and anencephaly, or shrunken brain.

Another new technique is thermography, which analyzes infrared (heat) radiation from the body. Variations in heat are revealed on graphs in varying shades of light and dark and can be used to confirm pregnancy very early in term (by picking up the tiny heat spot that is the developing fetus), to detect he presence of multiple fetuses, to determine the effects of various drugs on the fetus. And, again, this is done without radiation risk.

To monitor the health of the fetus during its long gestation period, doctors use electrocardiograph machines to pick up fetal heart beat. This is done simply by placing electrodes on the mother's abdomen. Heart beat can be detected as early as eleven weeks into pregnancy. A particularly critical time in gestation comes just before and during birth. It is at this point that the fetus is most vulnerable, that it is most likely, among other things, to suffer brain damage from lack of oxygen. That is why more and more doctors are using increasingly complex monitoring units during labor. These units tell them whether the fetus is in distress, permitting them to perform Cesarean sections in plenty of time if necessary. On the other hand, they also help prevent *unnecessary* Cesarean sections that are sometimes performed as a precaution by some doctors who have only rather subjective data to go on. They provide objective information on the status of the fetus and help take the guesswork out of the doctor's task.

One of the most advanced of these units was recently unveiled by Dr. Edward H. Hon of the Yale-New Haven Medical Center. His "intensive-care unit" can monitor four babies and their mothers at one time. Dr. Hon inserts a hollow tube through the mouth of the womb in each of his patients and then slips a small silver electrode through this so that it attaches itself to the scalp or arm of the fetus, whichever presents itself first. The electrode picks up fetal heart beat and sends back to the main unit a highly accurate record of this. If the fetus should become entangled in the umbilical cord, if the cord itself should become twisted or if the fetus should be getting an insufficient supply of oxygen, the electrode will immediately detect this and alert the doctor via visual readouts on the intensive-care unit. Another measuring device, similarly inserted into the uterus, provides physicians for the first time with highly precise information on the rate and intensity of the mother's labor contractions.

Such monitoring devices can be particularly valuable in the case of women with histories of difficult labor. Dr. Hon reports that in four hundred such difficult cases, where the intensive-care units were used, *none* of the babies died. Brain damage and other injuries were cut by 50 per cent (comparing this group to a similar group of four hundred, none of which had benefit of the monitoring units), and the number of Cesarean sections, which, of course, always carry some risk, was reduced by 75 per cent.

The one technique that tells doctors more about the health of the fetus than any other, however, is amniotic-fluid analysis or amniocentesis. This technique, like fetal surgery, got its start with the Rh problem, but has since gone on to find applications in the detection of a great many fetal ills.

Amniocentesis is a simple but not quite yet routine procedure. It involves pushing a needle through the abdominal wall of the mother and into the amniotic sac surrounding the fetus. Fluid is then aspirated into a syringe and the needle withdrawn. It is almost painless and only rarely results in any sort of complications. Most doctors perform the procedure, when indicated by histories of hereditary disease, Rh problems, difficult pregnancies, etc., between the twelfth and fourteenth weeks of gestation. This is because the enzymes, which carry out critical tasks inside the cells, are most active during this period.

By examining cells cultured from the amniotic fluid (the cells slough off the fetus), doctors can determine a great many things, including the sex of the baby. This is done by looking for the sex chromatin mass, a black spot that appears only in female cells. More important, fetologists, by examining these cells under the microscope, can detect all disorders that result from extra, broken or missing chromosomes. If the cells exhibit forty-seven chromosomes rather than the normal forty-six, for example, doctors will know that it is suffering from mongolism and will be severely retarded. If some of the chromosomes display a specific type of breakage, experienced geneticists can even detect probable damage from LSD ingestion or other drugs. In addition, they can discover fully one third of all defects that result in diseases of metabolism and body chemistry. And because cell examination reveals the sex of the fetus, they can often detect sex-linked hereditary diseases. If the mother carries the hemophilia or muscular dystrophy genes, for example, they can warn that her fetus, if it is a male, will have a 50 per cent chance of suffering these disabling diseases (even though the mother herself does not suffer from them).

Of course, once the mother learns that she is carrying a baby that will be either deformed or retarded, she faces the agonizing dilemma of whether to bear a defective or seek a therapeutic abortion. Columbia's Dr. Karlis Adamsons, a pioneering fetologist, invariably tries to persuade the mother to opt for the latter. "If necessary," he says, "we will take the mother to visit a group of incompetents [mongoloids and other retarded or deformed children] to help her realize what will happen if she insists on going through with the pregnancy."

Ironically, fetology sometimes stands in the way of a desired and, by many standards, justified abortion. Take the case of Mrs. James, the wife of a New York policeman, who suffered five painfully complicated pregnancies, three of them ending in stillbirth. She had already made arrangements to undergo sterilization when she learned that she was pregnant again.

"I just couldn't stand it," she said, weeping as she recalled the anguish of receiving what might otherwise have been joyous news. "I couldn't stand the thought of another stillbirth. I begged for an abortion, but because of this new technique [amniocentesis], the doctors felt they had to try to save the baby. I cried every night, and to tell the truth I was ready to die." Though intrauterine transfusions were necessary, the baby was delivered in good health. Mrs. James, while pleased to have an undamaged baby, still wondered why the doctors considered the patient inside her more important than herself.

Even the woman whose fetus medicine can now confirm as defective may not get an abortion easily. Mrs. Perry suddenly found herself pregnant at forty-five. "It was unplanned," this New Jersey housewife recalls, "but after I thought about it, it didn't seem like such a bad idea after all. That is until some of my friends told me that my chances of having a mongoloid child were frighteningly increased by virtue of my age." Mrs. Perry was referred to Dr. Cherry who performed an amniotic tap to see if the fetus was genetically sound. Already six months pregnant at this point, Mrs. Perry knew that it would be difficult to get a doctor to perform an abortion—*if* her fears materialized. While she waited for the results to come in on the amniotic tap, she called doctors all over the country and found that none wanted to perform an abortion on a fetus that old, no matter what.

Happily, Dr. Cherry reported that the fetus was healthy and normal in every respect. But Mrs. Perry was still shaken. "What good are all these advances," she asked, "if a woman finds out that her baby is going to be an idiot and then can't get an abortion?" More and more state legislatures are being confronted by such questions—and they are questions that urgently need answering. At present, only Colorado, North Carolina, Georgia, Arkansas, Kansas, Maryland, Oregon, Delaware, New Mexico and Hawaii authorize abortions if the fetus is demonstrated to be defective.

In some states, of course, hospital abortion boards interpret the law liberally (abortions have been performed at hospitals in New York, for example, for what was thought to be LSD-caused chromosome breakage), but very clearly, the diagnostic advances of fetology call for new guidelines. Geneticists Harold P. Klinger and Orlando J. Miller told an international symposium on fetology that all of the breakthrough in chromosome analysis "will be of limited significance if more liberalized medical abortion laws are not instituted in the United States."

Beyond this, they suggested that a national registry of hereditary abnormalities be established so that society can reap the full benefits of these new techniques. If such a registry were established, it would probably work something like this:

At birth, skin or blood samples would, as a matter of course, and, indeed, as a matter of law, be fed into a computerized genetic scanner. The scanner would quickly establish the presence of any chromosomal anomalies and print them out on data cards that would be kept on permanent file in Washington D.C. When two people apply for a marriage license, their respective cards would again be scanned—this time in conjunction with one another. They would then be issued an advisory telling them whether they are genetically compatible and what the odds are of their having abnormal children.

A number of scientists, including Nobel laureates Sir Peter Medawar, Francis Crick and Linus Pauling, believe that incompatible persons should be restrained by law from marrying one another or, in any event, from having children with one another. Dr. Pauling has suggested, only half in jest, that people who carry defective genes should have that information tattooed on their foreheads.

When I pointed out some of the possible advantages of a national registry of hereditary abnormalities on a New York radio show, the program's host expressed his amazement and shock, protesting that such an "invasion of privacy" would "take all the love out of marriage and certainly out of having children." And he went on to say that "when you meet an attractive girl it's all right to be curious about her figure, but to ask about her genes—that would be awful!"

This is an understandable emotional reaction and one that is registered by most individuals when they are first exposed to the notion of genetic scanning and typing. But it's also a reaction that generally fades with a little reflection. Having your genes analyzed by a computer is, in the first place, no more an "invasion of privacy" than having your heart beat analyzed by a doctor with a stethoscope. Nor is it any more an invasion of privacy than having your urine tested for glucose, your blood tested for venereal disease (already required almost everywhere in order to get a marriage license). All of these things are done for the good of ourselves and for the protection of society.

As for the idea that concern about genes takes all the love out of having children, this is nonsense. Surely the individual who takes the time and effort to ensure that any children he might have with a particular mate will be healthy and whole exhibits far more love for his offspring than does the individual who scorns such precautions as too "calculating" and unromantic. As one geneticist has put it, "There is nothing very romantic about a mongoloid child, a cleft palate or a deformed body."

With the advent of genetic typing, girl watching may be in for some new twists as red-blooded voyeurs begin showing as much interest in internal dimensions as they presently exhibit for external ones. "I love her but our number 11 chromosomes clash" could be the stuff of tragedy—and soap opera—in the very near future.

# II.

---

# BRAVE NEW
# BABY *TOMORROW*

Sex selection, embryo implants, fetal surgery —all of these are realities *now*. But though they make a dazzling repertoire in themselves, they are only shadows of what we can expect *tomorrow,* in five, ten, fifteen years, certainly by the end of the century, only thirty years distant.

As science gains ever increasing knowledge of and access to the developing and malleable fetus, to the primal cells of life (the egg and the sperm) and, most important, to the far tinier threads of life, hitherto so elusive, a new world of possibilities will unfold, a world of utopian promise—and untold peril. As the "predestinators" of Aldous Huxley's prophetic fiction *(Brave New World)* materialize in the form of white-frocked lab technicians who tend test-tube babies by day and play cards and go to the movies like everybody else at night, society is going to have to make a number of jolting adjustments. When man assumes— some might say *presumes*—powers previously held to be the exclusive province of God and nature, society will be forced, at the very least, to provide new definitions of God and man, perhaps to conclude, in a flash of irresistible hubris, that they are one and the same, or even that the latter has eclipsed the former.

Chapter One of this section—"Test-Tube Babies/

Test-Tube Mothers"—goes beyond mere fetal surgery and the momentary manipulation of life-before-birth to explore the possibilities of *complete* "ectogenesis," or test-tube pregnancy, from the moment of conception to the moment of "birth" (if that word will still apply in the days of glass and steel wombs). Chapter Two —"Genetic Engineering: From Man to Superman"— envisions man, building on knowledge and techniques already available, controlling life at its very roots, very possibly remodeling man for new environments, creating new life forms to fill specific needs, deleting undesirable genes and inserting new ones to make man anew—this time in the image of . . . well, if we're lucky, some objective, carefully selected and highly qualified committee charged with the task of engendering the ideal genotype, or if we're not, perhaps whoever happens to be in charge of things at the time.

The final chapter of this section—"Cloning: How to Have a Thousand Identical Twins"—describes what is probably the most bizarre, though also one of the most important, of the many biological perturbations that lie in store for us. Cloning, which is likely to be a *human* reality long before genetic surgery is refined to the point where parents can order blue eyes—and if they like, a prehensile tail—for their next child, is an asexual means of propagation. It has already been achieved in plants and some animals—through human intervention—in which the offspring in any given case have only *one* parent. That one parent can be male *or* female, and its offspring, more remarkable yet, will always be precisely identical in every detail, not only to one another but also to their single parent! Not all scientists welcome the advent of human cloning, though most believe that it is coming. What the development will entail, in terms of its applications, its abuse potential and so on, is discussed in this chapter— along with a review of the progress that has been realized to date.

# ONE

# Test-Tube Babies/ Test-Tube Mothers

With the advent of test-tube babies, Dr. Jean Rostand said, "It will be little more than a game to change the subject's sex, the color of its eyes, the general proportions of body and limbs, and perhaps the facial features." Moreover, when we learn enough about pregnancy to adequately imitate its various "life-support systems" and bring a fetus to term in a test tube, he said, the "man-farming biologist" may even be able to double the intellectual capacity of the fetus through chemical stimulation of the brain.

But could the baby factory of *Brave New World* ever materialize? Is ectogenesis, or test-tube pregnancy, in any sense possible? Actually, one of the most critical phases of ectogenesis—conception—has *already* been husbanded outside the human body. Before hurtling headlong into the laboratories of the men—some have called them "monsters"—who achieved this, first consider the complexities of conception, even as it occurs naturally:

To begin with there is the preparation of the sperm and the eggs. At birth, a baby girl's ovaries contain more than half a million egg cells. This, obviously, is more than she will ever have use for. In fact, not more than five hundred of these will ever mature to be released—one each month—from her ovaries during her lifetime. Why there are so many remains one of the great mysteries of medical science.

Generally, though not always, the process of ovulation or egg production alternates between left and right ovary on a monthly cycle. Usually a week to twelve days after the woman's menstrual period there is an eruption from the surface of the ovary of a little follicle. This watery blister bursts open—sometimes causing a perceptible twinge of pain—and the egg that it contains tumbles out and is caught by the lacy fimbriae or fingers of the fallopian tube. These finger-like structures draw the egg—no bigger than the point of a pin—into the tube. At this point, the egg, the nucleus of which resembles in color and shape the yolk of a chicken's egg, is encased in a gelatinous mass of four thousand to five thousand "nurse" cells, which nourish and protect it during its first vulnerable hours outside the ovary.

As the egg gently bounces down the four-inch fallopian tube, propelled by hairlike "cilia" that wave like tall grass in a soft breeze, the nurse cells gradually slough off and are dissolved by enzymes. At this point, the placid egg is ready to meet her mate: the sperm cell, which, as we are about to see, is anything but placid.

During intercourse, the male, on the average, ejaculates four hundred million sperm cells into the vagina. While the egg is more than 1/250 of an inch in diameter, the main body of the sperm is a mere 1/8000 of an inch across, and its volume is only 1/50,000 that of the egg. It has been estimated that all of the sperm necessary to produce the next generation in the United States could be contained in the space of a pinhead, while the eggs necessary for the same job would fill a pint jar. Why does the male produce and release so many of these microscopic creatures? Here we do know the answer—or part of it. It is primarily because the vaginal environment is so hostile to the sperm cells, which, incidentally, are the smallest of all the body's cells. They die off by the

millions shortly after they are released, slaughtered by
the acid that abounds in the vagina.

Sperm cells resemble tadpoles with their rounded
heads and long, whiplike tails, which they use for
propulsion, speeding—and considering their size that's
an accurate description—through the vaginal and cervical secretions at one-tenth inch per minute. Taking
their size into account, again, the seven-inch journey
through the birth canal and womb to the waiting egg
is equivalent to a five hundred-mile upstream swim for
a salmon! Yet they often make this hazardous journey
in under an hour, more than earning their title as the
"most powerful and rapid living creatures on earth."

Only the fittest survive to pass through the cervix
and into the womb. Once there, they find a more hospitable environment, more alkaline than acidic. Still,
many die along the way; others smash into the back of
the womb or go up the wrong fallopian tube. Many of
those that go up the correct one will miss the egg anyway, if only by a millionth of an inch. The idea that
the egg exerts some magical power of attraction has
been largely disproved. Those that hit the egg—and
there are thousands of them that make it—do so
blindly. Soon the egg resembles a pincushion, except
that in this case the "pins" beat their tails furiously
trying to drill into the egg. This is a sight (which can
be seen with a proper microscope) never to be forgotten. Dr. Shettles, whose work was discussed in Part
One, was one of the first to photograph the drama,
which he calls "the dance of love."

Under the microscope, one can see the sperm making heroic efforts to gain admittance to the egg's inner
sanctum, which contains the nucleus and the chromosomes. Many are able to break through the egg's outer
core, but *only one* penetrates into the interior, tail and
all, there to merge with the egg's nucleus and create a
new human being. As soon as one sperm penetrates
the nucleus, all others find the way to the heart of the
egg forever blocked. Some unexplained mechanism
within the egg apparently releases a chemical that ren-

ders the innermost portions of it absolutely impregnable once it has been fertilized by a single sperm. Hence the egg's unsuccessful "suitors" wear themselves out "pounding at the door," as Dr. Shettles put it, and then finally die of exhaustion.

The sperm carries twenty-three chromosomes and so does the egg. Twenty-two of these (in each) match up as pairs that determine (with the help of the much smaller genes and nucleotides which make them up) all the bodily characteristics of the new individual—except for sex. The two remaining chromosomes decide the subject's sex. The female always contributes an X chromosome. If the sperm that penetrates the ovum also carries an X chromosome then the resulting individual will be XX, otherwise known as a girl. But if the sperm carries the Y chromosome, the baby will be XY, which, to the geneticist, spells b-o-y.

That's conception *a la* Mother Nature, complex indeed. And yet man has already successfully mimicked this part of her act. Dr. John Rock, the famed Harvard gynecologist who was one of the three developers of the birth-control pill, was the first to succeed. He obtained ripe eggs from female patients and then exposed them to sperm cells in the test tube. No special medium was used to prepare the cells, and success was slight. Only with the sperm of one man did Dr. Rock succeed in fertilizing any of the eggs—and then they died anyway after the first cell divisions. Still, this was a start. Dr. Rock proved that it could be done —and this was way back in the 1940s.

In the 1950s, Dr. Shettles repeated Dr. Rock's experiments, but he went to pains to "trick" the germinal cells into thinking that they were in normal surroundings inside the female body by bathing them in a carefully prepared solution consisting, in part, of natural cervical secretions. In this way, Dr. Shettles repeatedly achieved *in vitro* (meaning "in glass" or test tube) fertilization of the human egg. He maintained one of his "test-tube babies" for six days—the point at which it would normally attach itself to the lining of the uterus. Embryo implant techniques had not yet been devised in the 1950s (and, as was noted in Part One, are only now about to be applied to humans), so Dr. Shettles had no choice but to abandon the tiny embryo he had created.

Segments of society damned him for this. Some editorialists of the religious press screamed, "Monster!" The Pope took the occasion of Dr. Shettles' attendance at the International Fertility Conference in Italy in 1954 to condemn those who "take the Lord's work" into their own hands. Dr. Shettles, however, was convinced that the work he was doing in the 1950s was both necessary and important and so continued for a time with this research, contributing substantially in the process to the study of human embryology. Thanks to the photographic record he made of his work, students for the first time were able to study *directly* the development of man from the moment of conception onward. Today, Dr. Shettles' photographs (or micrographs as they are known)—many of them considered classics—appear in his biological atlas *Ovum Humanum,* in more than fifty textbooks on embryology, biology and genetics, and in enlarged form hang in the American Museum of Natural History in New York, in the Museum of Science in Boston and in the Academy of Sciences in Moscow.

Looking back on the furor that his work unleashed, Dr. Shettles is fond of recalling "the nice, little old ladies" who inquired so frequently about the origin of the human eggs he used in his experiments. "Most of them I just poached," he would say. As for his scruples about growing a test-tube baby into a mature adult: "I have none," he says, smiling. "There's nothing I'd like better than to grow a beautiful lab assistant."

As it turned out, Dr. Shettles moved on to a different field of research in the 1960s—that of sex selection. But others have carried on where he left off. Among them was Dr. Danielle Petrucci of Bologna, Italy. In the early 1960s, Dr. Petrucci and his colleagues, Dr. Laura de Pauli and Raffaele Bernaboo, nurtured human egg cells in tiny glass "wombs," which they maintained at a constant temperature of 97.7 degrees F. Sperm was introduced into the minuscule wombs by way of capillary action. Once fertilization had taken place, verifiable by microscopic examination of the eggs while still in their "wombs" (hollowed-out depressions in glass slides), the team of doctors immersed the resulting embryos in oxygenated amniotic fluid obtained from pregnant women.

Dr. Petrucci set off a new controversy when he announced to the world that he had grown one of his test-tube creations from a microscopic speck to the size of a pea (about twenty-nine days into gestation). Another lived for fifty-nine days. The experiments horrified the Catholic world in particular, and the Pope condemned Dr. Petrucci, himself a Catholic, forcing him to curtail further research.

The gap between science and society was suddenly exposed—and raw-edged, as evidenced by this anguished, but misdirected, volley from *America*, a leading Catholic journal: "The spirit of Frankenstein did not die with the Third Reich. His blood brothers regard a human being as just another expendable microbe, provided it is legally defenseless, physically helpless, and tiny enough to ride on the stage of a microscope." Others rushed in to join in the condemnation. *L'Osservatore Romano*, a newspaper that frequently serves as one of the voices of the Vatican, said the experiments were sacrilegious, as did Radio Vatican. One leading Italian geneticist, Dr. Luigi Gedda, said, "Experiments of this kind do not take into due account the spiritual values of the human being."

*America*, despite its hyperbole, made some legitimate points. "The human person is a sacredness hedged round by a mantle of dignity and inviolability no matter whether it is cradled in a father's arms, nestled in a mother's womb, or floats in a test tube at the threshold of visibility," its editors declared, holding to the traditional notion of the Catholic Church that life begins at the moment of fertilization, a notion that may before too long give way, even within the Church, to the idea that life begins at the moment of nidation —when the embryo attaches itself to the lining of the womb.

Whatever takes place in this regard, however, there were yet other, perhaps better, objections to the experiments. "The experimenter who creates human life in a test tube," *America* contended, "deliberately places a person in an environment where the most basic and vital requirements of human nature cannot conceivably be met in the current state of medical science. To produce a human being, holding it captive like a genie in a bottle, and doom it to inevitable death is to exercise an irresponsible dominion that cannot be justified by any appeal to the common welfare of mankind or to the advancement of scientific goals."

Those who disagree with these arguments—and particularly with the idea that even a few embryos should not be sacrificed in the effort to improve the lot of *all* mankind—will be heartened to learn that a team of doctors at Oxford University recently made public their success in achieving test-tube fertilization of human eggs and their intentions to continue with the research.

Others, while generally approving of the ultimate aims of this research, may continue to be worried by the question: Is science able to cope with the requirements of the test-tube baby, once it is created? The answer, quite clearly, is no—not at the present time. But researchers are aggressively accepting the challenge on several fronts.

Scientists have developed the frozen-sperm, egg and embryo banks that could be used to supply the "baby factories" of tomorrow, to keep the embryos in "suspension" (but very much alive) until there was some demand for them. Once thawed out, however (and if not scheduled for implantation into a natural womb), the trouble begins. Artificial wombs of the Petrucci stripe simply aren't adequate to support a developing fetus over a nine-month period. One of the most pressing needs, then, is for an artificial placenta, the computerlike organ that regulates the complex exchange of nutrients, oxygen and so on between mother and fetus.

Fortunately, researchers in Britain, the United States and the Soviet Union are all actively trying to develop just such a system. The immediate need for an artificial placenta arises from the fact that prematurity—birth before term—remains the number-one killer of infants. With this to goad them on, medical researchers are bound to come up with an adequate system before too long. As the journal *New Scientist* puts it, "The development of the 'perfect' artificial placenta can only be a matter of time."

In Britain, researchers at King's College have had some success with a machine designed to keep premature babies alive by regulating blood components, including oxygen. A far more complex machine, designed to control the exchange of liquid and solids, as well as gases, is under development at Cambridge University. It is believed that the Soviet Academy of Medical Sciences, which has been concerned with the development of artificial placentas and artificial wombs for many years, may be at the forefront of this research. Considerable success has been intimated but as yet no details of the work have been forthcoming.

In the United States, Dr. Kermit Krantz of the University of Kansas Medical Center has developed a machine that simulates placental exchange of substances between the mother and fetus. It is capable of supplying the fetus with oxygen, hormones, food and antibodies. It is also able to remove wastes. Dr. Krantz has been quoted as saying that "It's not hard to see how any malfunction of the placenta could turn a potential Einstein into a mediocrity. If we learn enough —who knows?—maybe we can turn mediocrities into Einsteins."

A complete artificial womb, which resembled a small, steel bathysphere, complete with porthole (it was called "a womb with a view"), was constructed a few years ago by Dr. Robert Goodlin of the Stanford University School of Medicine. Dr. Goodlin was able to keep one ten-week-old fetus alive for a few hours inside the device, which was filled with an oxygenated saline solution similar to the natural amniotic fluid that surrounds the fetus in a natural womb. Dr. Goodlin successfully oxygenated the fetus by forcing the gas through the baby's skin. This was done by putting the oxygen-laden saline solution under twenty-two pounds' pressure. He failed however to force out the carbon dioxide wastes; hence the fetus died.

Dr. Goodlin was ultimately forced to terminate his research for lack of adequate funding. But now the National Institutes of Health, financially better prepared for such a project, are attempting to develop an artificial womb. They have already successfully maintained animal fetuses (lambs) for periods exceeding two days. The artificial placenta portion features a blood oxygenator developed by Dr. Theodor Kolobow. It is, essentially, an artificial lung with a spiral coil membrane that perfuses the blood with oxygen. The womb itself is designed to hold—and control—a synthetic amniotic fluid in which the fetus is immersed. The oxygenator is now being tested on newborn human infants who suffer from respiratory distress due to prematurity, and the first attempts to sustain fetuses in total perfusion within the artificial womb have been termed successful, though refinements are certainly needed before this portion of the system can be applied to human fetuses. All in all, an impressive start.

Once it is possible to bring a baby to term in the laboratory, can one legitimately object any longer to the sort of *in vitro* fertilization procedures developed by Drs. Rock, Shettles and Petrucci, among others? In Aldous Huxley's *Brave New World,* society embraces the test-tube mother and maligns the natural one. Indeed, the very word "mother" is studiously avoided, as if it were imbued with a rather bad odor, if not actually an obscenity. In the world Huxley envisions, people recall the old days in which babies were ejected from a woman's womb with revulsion. The pain, blood and agony of pregnancy and birth, as suffered in the previous era, are all the proof the Brave New Worlders need that they have pulled themselves up from their barbarous origins into a greater day—a day in which babies are produced on an assembly line in a fully automated "factory." In this day women suffer no more from pregnancy and birth than do men.

Many would argue, quite rationally, that that is as it should be. This is a particularly prevalent argument now that women's liberation movements are proliferating everywhere. The old order of nature that dictated that the woman would stay close to the bower, there to breed, bear and tend the brood, while the man went forth to forage, hunt and bring home the bread, has long since fallen by the way. Its echo lingers on but is becoming increasingly faint. It seems apparent, at any rate, that many women, even without any coercion from the state, would avail themselves of the services of the test-tube mother as soon as they were proffered, eagerly forgoing the rigors of pregnancy by dropping off at the baby factory their two- or three-day-old embryos for predestination, gestation and decanting. Along the nine-month way, they could drop in at the laboratory to check on their babies' progress, perhaps ordering a few changes here and there. The "coming out" party could well take on a whole new meaning as proud parents and their friends gather at the mouth of glass-and-steel wombs for the "birth" of their babies, once they've reached term.

Apart from the considerable advantages of freeing women from pregnancy, ectogenesis holds out the promise of better health and a stronger, better formed body for the fetus. Instead of having to resort to sophisticated and dangerous fetal surgery, doctors of tomorrow will have only to dip into an artificial womb (as simple as opening or closing a door) in order to treat the fetus and even change its physical and mental characteristics.

The fetus, because it is so malleable, can easily be manipulated and thus changed in a variety of ways. Dr. O. S. Heyns of the University of Witwatersrand in South Africa, for example, has claimed sensational results with a technique devised to enhance the intelligence of the fetus. The technique entails placing pregnant women in decompression chambers at various times during the last half of their pregnancies. The procedure reportedly provides the fetus with an unusual amount of oxygen. Dr. Heyns reports that babies who had benefit of the technique proved after birth to be of exceptional intelligence; many could carry on coherent conversations at eighteen months, and one was speaking fluently in four languages by the age of three. It appears that if too little oxygen can cause mental retardation—and that is certainly an established fact—"too much" may result in the opposite. Researchers at the Yerkes Primate Center in Atlanta are now exploring the possibilities of giving the procedure a full experimental testing. If the procedure works as well as Dr. Heyns and his colleagues claim—on the unexposed fetus—think how much better it might work on a test-tube baby whose responses to various oxygen doses could be directly studied and measured as one went along.

It was Dr. Rostand who suggested something even more startling. When test-tube pregnancy becomes a reality, he asked, "Is it very rash to imagine that it would be possible to increase the number of brain cells in the human member? A young embryo has already in the cerebral cortex the nine billion pyramidal cells which will condition its mental activity during the whole of its life. This number, which is reached by geometrical progression or simple doubling, after thirty-three divisions of each cell (two, four, eight, sixteen, thirty-two and so on), could in turn be doubled if we succeeded in causing just one more division—the thirty-fourth." This, he proposed, might easily be accomplished by the chemical stimulation of the brain at the appropriate moment during test-tube gestation. He acknowledged that this would increase the size of the brain and the head significantly and thus would not be practical for normal birth within a natural womb. The enlarged head would harm the mother and make passage through the birth canal impossible. But why should intellect be governed, in part, by the size of a woman's pelvis, Dr. Rostand asked, pointing out that an artificial womb could have a "mouth" of unlimited size. And the rest of the body, he said, could similarly be "engineered" by doctors with easy access to the fetus so that it would be proportionate with the larger head.

That chemical intervention in fetal development can have dramatic results has been amply demonstrated by doctors concerned with yet another aspect of bodily development: sex. Researchers in many parts of the world have induced laboratory animals to undergo complete sexual transformations via chemical engineering. Again, because the fetus is so malleable, many scientists reasoned that it might easily be encouraged to disregard its genetic sex. Some of them wondered whether a simple injection of hormones or hormone suppressants during fetal development might not result in sexual change. Though this has not yet been tried on the human fetus, one can get a good idea of its effects by looking at some of the animal experiments.

German scientists injected a chemical that neutralizes the male sex hormone into pregnant rats. Male offspring were born with vaginas and after being castrated and implanted with ovaries became functioning females, capable of reproduction. Dr. Rostand reported that in other animal experiments, chemicals injected during the very earliest stages of embryonic development resulted in *complete* sexual reversals: embryos originally destined to be females turned out at birth to be perfectly formed males and vice versa. "Using salamanders and toads," Dr. Rostand said, "false females [meaning that they were genetic males transformed by hormones] have been coupled with true males and false males with true females, and from these unions descendants have been obtained that were the issue of two fathers or two mothers." These "homosexual unions," as Dr. Rostand called them, resulted when male parents were involved only in male offspring and, in the other instance, in female offspring. Again, this is the sort of radical manipulation that will be greatly facilitated according to Dr. Rostand, with the advent of test-tube pregnancy.

Recall, too, as Dr. Myers pointed out, that the early fetus will readily accept skin and tissue grafts since it has not yet developed an immunological system of its own. Thus, the man-farming biologist, as Dr. Rostand calls him, will find it relatively easy to perform transplant operations of his test-tube patients that would otherwise be severely complicated by the rejection phenomenon. Experiments carried out by the Nobelist Dr. Peter Medawar suggest that it may even be possible to treat the fetus in such a way—at just the right moment during gestation—that much later in life it will tolerate tissue grafts and organ transplants should such ever become necessary without any difficulty whatever.

Incredible as some of these prospects are, they are not incredible enough to suit some people. In the course of a radio discussion on the "Biological Revolution" not long ago, relatively easy to perform transplant operations on his test-tube baby is not something you start with sperm and egg; you've got to start from scratch." By starting "from scratch," presumably he meant from the chemical bases of life, from the combination of the various "ingredients" of life. The synthesization of life in this manner would have to rank as the most stunning accomplishment ever achieved by man, yet there are many who think that it is within our grasp. Certainly, man has dreamed about assuming the God-like capability of creating life in the laboratory for centuries, at least since the days of the alchemists.

That this dream has become even more compelling

in the present time is not surprising, in light of contemporary discoveries about the probable origins of life on this planet. It was in the early 1950s that Dr. Harold Urey, a Nobel Prize winner, proposed an experiment that was to provide science with an explanation of the way in which life, in all likelihood, emerged for the first time from the chemical constituents of the planet more than two thousand million years ago. Dr. Urey argued convincingly that the earth's atmosphere originally consisted of only relatively simple gases such as ammonia, methane, hydrogen and water vapor. He pointed out that amino acids, which go into making up protein, essential to all living matter, are constructed around ammonia molecules. It seemed to Dr. Urey that the combination of gases that was most likely to have characterized the earth's atmosphere during its earliest history, when exposed to abundant ultraviolet radiation, would give rise to the amino acids that are the building blocks of life. Our present atmosphere, replete with oxygen produced by living things, screens out much of the naturally occurring ultraviolet radiation. But the sort of early atmosphere envisioned by Dr. Urey would have transmitted a great deal of ultraviolet light.

Hence the stage was set for the experiment: Simply reproduce in the laboratory these primal conditions and see if they give rise to amino acids. In 1953, Stanley Miller, one of Dr. Urey's students, undertook the experiment. As predicted by Dr. Urey, the gases that were exposed to the radiation produced the amino acids. Subsequently, variations on this experiment have demonstrated how other essential components of life, including the nucleotide units of the nucleic acids, proteins and so on, can construct themselves in nature. One of the most stunning breakthroughs came in 1967 when clusters of organic molecules called "coacervates" and believed to be precursors of living cells were formed spontaneously in the laboratory by merely mixing different proteins, something that would surely have happened naturally, given the conditions that are said to have existed at the time when life first began evolving (which we know was at least two billion years ago, thanks to fossils that have been recovered and dated).

Since then other persuasive theories have been developed to explain how these cellular precursors evolved into full-fledged cells capable of trapping some of the sun's energy in order to supply the power needed to carry on their complex activities. So rapid have been the advances that Dr. Charles C. Price of the University of Pennsylvania declared in 1965 that "The synthesis of life is now within reach." Upon assuming his post as president of the American Chemical Society, he proposed that the synthetic creation of life be declared a national goal. With a crash effort, involving perhaps a quarter of the nation's scientific manpower, he said the goal could be realized in twenty years. He reasoned that such a goal should be at least as important to the nation as sending a man to the moon and in the long run would have far greater impact, permitting even the ultimate creation of new forms of life.

As will be demonstrated in the next chapter, impressive steps have already been taken toward attaining this goal, steps that promise to take evolution, once and for all, out of nature's hands and put it, for better or worse, into man's.

## TWO

# Genetic Engineering: From Man to Superman

A natural substance called deoxyribonucleic acid has given rise to a set of initials—DNA—that school children (and, increasingly, their parents) now regard with greater recognition and certainly with far more awe than they do such old standbys as FDR, LBJ and even LSD. DNA, which occupies the nucleus of every living cell, was first identified in the nineteenth century, though at that time no one had any inkling as to what function, if any, it might serve. Then, in the 1940s, it was finally established, in a series of experiments at the Rockefeller Institute, that it *does* serve a function and that, in fact, without it there would be no life, plant *or* animal, whatever on the planet. In short, it was demonstrated that DNA is the very essence of biological inner space, the chemical template of creation, the residing place of heredity, the blueprint of life—the paeans are still being sounded. DNA is the stuff of chromosomes, genes and nucleotides, the wondrously complex structures that determine not only the grosser characteristics of our being (whether four-legged, two-legged or no-legged) but also the finest and most intimate details (red wings, blue eyes, moles).

The delineation of the DNA structure in the 1950s —by Dr. Francis H. C. Crick and Dr. James Watson, both of whom have since been awarded the Nobel Prize for their achievement—and the illumination of many of its inner workings in the 1960s, primarily by Dr. Marshall Nirenberg, have truly set the stage for the premier performance of a new creator: Man. With the genetic code of life rapidly yielding its secrets to the decipherers, a new era is dawning in which man will have at his disposal the means of remaking himself in images limited perhaps only by his imagination or according to the dictates of a changing or new environment. Perhaps, as the world grows "smaller" due to the crush of population, man will find it advantageous to make *himself* smaller; as he moves into the oceans, perhaps he will want to incorporate gills and other aquatic appurtenances into his genotype; similarly, as he moves out into the far reaches of space, he may wish to redesign his body in such a way that he will be able to cope with the requirements of this new world without recourse to life-support systems designed at great costs in efficiency and mobility to reconcile incompatibilities of organism and environment. Manipulation of the DNA molecule or "genetic engineering" promises to make all of this—and much more—possible.

At an international symposium on "The Future of Man" held in London a few years ago, the world-renowned geneticist-philosopher Dr. J. B. S. Haldane looked ahead to the day when it will be possible to engineer man's characteristics according to the needs of society. Discoursing on the varied requirements of extraterrestrial environments, Dr. Haldane observed that "a gibbon is better preadapted than a man for life in a low gravitational field, such as that of a spaceship, an asteroid, or perhaps even the moon. A platyrhine with a prehensile tail is even more so. Gene grafting may make it possible to incorporate such features into the human stocks."

Dr. Haldane had other proposals. For long space journeys, he said, legs would be just so much dead weight, and it might be best to breed legless astronauts for the first spaceflight to the stars, "thus reducing not only their weight, but their food and oxygen requirements. A regressive mutation to the condition of our ancestors in the mid-Pliocene, with prehensile feet, no appreciable heels and an apelike pelvis, would be still better." For high-gravitational fields, such as will ultimately be encountered on planets like Jupiter, Dr. Haldane suggested that astronauts be bred for short legs and squat bodies. Perhaps, he said, they should even be quadrupedal! "I would back an achondroplasic [dwarf] against a normal man on Jupiter."

The late Dr. Olaf Stapledon envisioned Jupiter man in much the same way. He, too, proposed a four-legged man for high gravitational fields but went further, adding that such a man should also come equipped with a head set back over the forelegs for stability and protruding eyes designed for optimal vision. Dr. Stapledon also proposed for this descendant of man an elephantlike trunk with fingerlike projections for grasping.

Among other controlled mutations foreseen by Dr. Haldane is the "aseptic" man, germ-free inside and out. This future cousin, he declared could be a boon to germ-free planets but might otherwise prove troublesome, particularly whenever forced to come into contact with humans such as ourselves (who enjoy close symbiotic relationships with millions of external and internal microbes). "To an aseptic person, producing among other things inodorous feces," Dr. Haldane pointed out, "the rest of humanity will appear as stinkers and there will be grave emotional tensions, including a sexual barrier."

If this sounds like science fiction, recall that far more spectacular transformations take place *without* any intervention from man every day. We have grown so used to the notion that tadpoles develop into frogs, for example, and that caterpillars change into butterflies (incredibly different creatures in appearance) that we forget or simply never stop to think what remarkable transformations these are. Think of the formidable power of the chemicals that are responsible for these changes. The chemicals are the nucleic acids, the DNA that inhabits the nucleus of each cell in every living thing. Encoded within these microscopic molecules are the blueprints that guide these transformations, no matter how complex. "In the face of such natural phenomena," Dr. Dean E. Woolbridge states, "one wonders whether the fairy-tale conversion of Cinderella's white mice into footmen was so far-fetched after all!"

With the introduction of certain "gene-switching" chemicals or the manipulation of the DNA itself, man can tap and redirect some of this molecular power. Tiny doses of the chemical thyroxin, for example, will so alter the genetic controls of the Mexican axolotl, a gilled newt that is generally confined to the water, that it will suddenly forsake the environment that has been its home for thousands of years and take to the land under the convincing guise of a salamander. The transformation takes place in a very short time, generally no more than two or three weeks.

There are other examples of man's intervention into the molecular processes of life with similarly startling results. Dr. Jean Rostand has described experiments in which the genetic material is manipulated in such a way that animals can be induced, for example, to reproduce by parthenogenesis (without intercourse or male fertilization).

"It is now a regular thing," he noted, "for perfectly constituted living creatures to be born from a virgin egg without any help from a male, on condition that within the egg there has been produced a doubling of the chromosomes." Women, he predicted, may one day indulge regularly in this sort of "auto-adultery." Egg cells, in many cases, can be tricked into doubling themselves, usually by jolting them with chemicals; even pricking them with a pin sometimes sets them off. Ultimately it will be possible for women to fertilize their own eggs by injecting them with DNA from other cells in their own bodies, bringing the chromosomal complement to the required forty-six.

Dr. Rostand noted a number of variations on parthenogenesis that have already been achieved in the laboratory, resulting in creatures that he described as being of "somewhat baroque composition." A doubling of maternal chromosomes, for example, has been induced in *fertilized* eggs, resulting in offspring that, in Dr. Rostand's words, "must be considered their mother's children twice over and their father's only once."

French researchers in 1959 injected DNA extracted from a species of ducks known as Khaki Campbells into ducks of an entirely different species. It was their expectation that the offspring of the ducks thus treated might exhibit some of the characteristics of the Khaki Campbells. The results were nothing short of sensational. Even before any offspring came along the adult ducks *themselves* began to undergo extensive changes, taking on the markedly different characteristics of the Khaki Campbells. Their coloration changed and their necks began to assume the particular curve that distinguishes the Campbells.

Other transformations have been reported since then. Meanwhile, the means for manipulating the DNA molecules have been developing rapidly—so rapidly that many scientists are now predicting "genetic surgery" for the relatively near future. When that day comes genes will be excised and added at will, while others will undergo repair or modification, depending upon what the genetic engineers' designs are.

But how would genetic surgery—a term coined by the Nobelist Dr. Edward Tatum—be performed? The means of performing delicate operations on the genes are very nearly at hand. A procedure for injecting various substances into sperm and egg cells has been developed by Dr. Teh Ping Lin of San Francisco. The achievement was monumental because the eggs that Dr. Teh was working with in the late 1960s were microscopic. He "grasped" them by sucking them into an instrument called a "micropipette," a hairlike tube with an internal diameter of fifteen-thousandths of a millimeter. Then he inserted into this tiny tube a microsyringe only one-thousandth of a millimeter in diameter and with this injected his "patients" with a harmless substance. The eggs, in this case mice eggs, were then implanted in female mice and carried to term. A significant number of the fetuses proved normal at birth, demonstrating that this revolutionary technique can be used to introduce a variety of substances into the genetic matter at or even before conception.

An even more elegant approach to genetic surgery involves the use of viruses, things we generally think of as our enemies. They may, in fact, prove to be very good friends. The virus is usually described as a "quasi-living thing." It consists of a coat of protein and an inner core of nucleic acid—but nothing more. Unlike cells, it has none of the machinery necessary for metabolizing of food, expulsion of wastes and so on. To reproduce, it must invade other cells and "take over" their machinery. It does this by imposing its DNA on the nucleus of the cell, pre-empting there the original genetic message. The instructions this viral DNA sends out to the various working centers of the cell are always the same: Make more copies of the virus. And the cell always obeys, giving up its original duties to produce copies of its new master.

The mechanisms by which viruses are able to insinuate their ways into the cells are not fully understood but their ability to do so makes for some exciting prospects. Already scientists are working on ways of freighting viruses with engineered pay loads destined for biological inner space. Such viruses will provide ideal vehicles for the transport of missing genes or even of entirely new genes into the cells, genes designed to provide the incipient human being with new characteristics.

And what sort of viruses would be used? Eventually, perhaps, man-made ones or natural varieties that are able to get in and out of the cells with ease but do no damage in the process. Two such viruses are under intensive study now: the SV40 and Shope papilloma virus. Both infect man but do no detectable damage. Dr. Stanfield Rogers, a biochemist in cancer research at Oak Ridge National Laboratory, noted in *New Scientist* that "viruses such as these hold a tremendous potential for treating a wide variety of diseases. The genetic-deficiency diseases provide the most obvious example. If, for example, SV40 or the Shope virus carries information specifying the synthesis of phenylalanine hydroxylase, the enzyme that is missing in phenylketonuria (PKU), patients suffering from this disease could be genetically cured by adding this virus information to that of his genome." (PKU causes severe mental retardation and, frequently, death.)

Some viruses will not even require "engineering" in order to effect cures. The Shope virus, for example, may be used—as is—in the very near future to treat arginaemia, another genetic-deficiency disease, in which the genetic instructions for breaking down the amino acid arginine are missing. It happens that the DNA in the Shope virus contains these instructions and is able to reduce arginine levels in the blood without any undesirable side effects. Hence, if the disease can be diagnosed before irreversible damage sets in, the Shope virus may well provide a cure for arginaemia, which results in mental retardation, various metabolic abnormalities and epileptic-type symptoms.

Another disease that predisposes certain individuals to a particular type of skin cancer results from a deficiency in the genetic material. And this again is a deficiency that scientists believe can be eliminated by the introduction of a virus—possibly the SV40 virus. "Theoretically," Dr. Rogers observes, "there might be a specific genetic-deficiency disease relating to each individual enzyme in the metabolic pathways in the body. The number of these possibilities is thus huge. The problem is even more immense when looked at in the broader sense, *for all of our diseases (except those due to trauma), even the ubiquitous disease called 'aging,' are genetically conditioned* [italics mine.]. If we could specify the information needed, then many of these diseases might be cured or prevented by introducing the appropriate 'message' with a passenger virus."

Dr. Rogers concedes that it is "too much to expect that all the different sorts of information needed are carried fortuitously by the DNA or RNA of passenger viruses that occur in nature." Alternatives, however, are available. Dr. Rogers notes that it is possible to modify existing viruses by hybridizing them with other nucleic acids. Some of the viruses readily accept such "grafts," incorporating the new nucleotides (the small units that go into making up genes) into their structure.

Another—more exciting—possibility is the synthesis in the laboratory of the specific genetic information desired in any given case. Viruses and sizable DNA sequences, in fact, have already been "constructed" in the laboratory. It has been demonstrated that if you bring all the right "raw materials," that is, the individual components, of these molecules together in the test tube *they will assemble themselves,* forming molecules or viruses indistinguishable from those that occur in nature. Man has still not succeeded, however, in getting the raw materials to combine in completely new orders, but that is only a matter of time.

When fully refined, genetic surgery will probably employ techniques even more exotic than viral transduction. It has been suggested, for example, that microsurgical tools equipped with laser beams may be used to vaporize individual genes or even sections of the smaller nucleotides in an effort to eliminate specific defects. Dr. Tatum suggests that "repressor molecules" may also be developed to "erase" undesired genes or at least render them inoperative. To produce desirable genetic material in relatively large quantities, he envisions "enzyme xerography," in which enzymes are used to replicate the genes in whatever quantity is desired. Grafting of genetic material in mammalian cells, Dr. Tatum observes, is already underway.

Things are moving along so rapidly that Dr. Tatum declares that "We can be optimistic about long-range possibilities of therapy by the design and synthesis and introduction of new genes or gene products into cells of defective organs." Dr. Nirenberg says, "My guess is that cells will be programed with synthesized messages within twenty-five years. If efforts along these lines were intensified, bacteria might be programed within five years." Dr. Joshua Lederberg also predicts genetic surgery within the next ten or twenty years, perhaps sooner with an all-out effort.

Where will all this lead? Some of the possibilities—such as Dr. Haldane's engineered space mutants—have already been discussed. *Science Journal,* a British publication, asked its readers, most of them scientists, what they would do, given the opportunity to redesign the human body. One writer proposed that man be engineered in such a way that he could be coupled directly to a computer to enhance his efficiency. (See final chapter, "The Cyborg: Evolution to Machine—and Beyond.") A writer from Manchester University suggested that the human female be restructured in such a way that she would lay eggs, which could either be hatched "or eaten for breakfast." Others called for gills and other underwater apparatus, while some pointed to the utility of an enlarged caecum (the sac containing the vermiform appendix) containing bacteria able to transform cellulose into food. (Cows presently have this undeniably economical capability.)

One suggestion called for the complete suppression of the Y (male) chromosome and another for the separation of the esophagus from the trachea so that food won't go down the wrong passageway. One reader wanted everyone programed with photographic memories, and a female reader called for large fingers on one hand—for heavy work—and small, sensitive ones on the other for delicate work. Ear flaps analogous to eyelids (except in this case to shut out sound rather than light) were suggested by a reader tired of late-night parties in an adjacent apartment.

Many wanted improved vision, suggesting that heads should be constructed in such a way that they could swivel through 180 degrees. Some wanted protruding eyes, eyes on stalks and even an eye on the tip of the index finger. One reader said the vulnerable male testes should be tucked inside the body. Another proposed orifices at the waist for exhalation of air. This, he said, would make for better respiratory exchange and noted that the circulation of air under the clothing would reduce bodily heat loss. One of the most intriguing proposals called for all aging (beyond the completion of the maturation process) to occur suddenly—over the last three days of an individual's life. (See Chapter Two of Part Three, "The Scientific Quest for Immortality.")

Still other suggestions for the remaking of man were forthcoming recently in *Sciences,* a publication of the New York Academy of Sciences. Among them was one by Dr. Charles H. Townes, the Nobel Prize-winning physicist who developed the principles underlying development of the laser. "Man should be smaller in size," he said, "and have a much longer life cycle than in the past. . . . In the past, man's size needed to be reasonably large so that he could exert the physical force necessary to do work and fight enemies; the application of intelligence and the development of tools has completely changed this. . . . Small size and long life would, of course, very much facilitate long space journeys, to mention one of man's most recent challenges."

Dr. Dominic Recaldin of London University had an ingenuous plan for future man: "We should take a lesson in self-sufficiency from the plants," he wrote, "and learn the art of photosynthesis before our greedy teeth pick the planet clean." (Photosynthesis is the process by which green plants convert sunlight into chemical energy such as sugar and protein.) "With chlorophyll beneath their skins, men could unchain themselves forever from the soil. . . . Not only would they learn to laugh in famine's face, but they would kick the color problem, too. Whoever heard of a master race of Anglo-Saxon, Protestant Jolly Green Giants?"

The possibilities, it should be apparent by now, are limited only by our imaginations. As man moves out into new frontiers, he may find it not only desirable, but necessary to change himself in a variety of ways. If we are ever to move under water, we will have to assume the ability to breathe with gills and perhaps communicate by sonar—like porpoises. Or like bees, we may find it helpful to extend our vision to parts of the spectrum presently invisible to us or our hearing to ranges presently beyond our reach. On long space journeys it may be essential that we be able to hibernate like the hedgehog and regenerate lost or damaged limbs like the newt.

As for sex, we have only to look around us to get some grasp of the incredible possibilities. The animal kingdom is full of creatures whose sexual adaptability far outstrips our own. Take the slipper limpet, for example, a form of marine life common in the Atlantic. It starts out life without any sex whatever, grows into a male and then into a hermaphrodite (possessing both male and female sex organs) before finally ending life as a female. The most interesting thing about the slipper limpet is its tendency to remain male as long as there is an adequate supply of females in the vicinity. It is only when there is a shortage that it will throw in the towel, make the sacrifice and transform itself into a female. Other creatures, particularly of the annelid variety, exhibit an ability to change sex repeatedly, in order to cope with constantly changing conditions around them.

"Even in such advanced creatures as the bony fish," writes Dr. Peter Scott in *New Scientist*, "some individuals of some species can function as females while

they are young, and as males later on, while others
are normally hermaphroditic and may even fertilize
their own eggs. Different species also show an expedi-
ent ability to advance or retard the onset of sexual
maturity, so that some are born with mature testes
and may mate within two days of birth. Eels may
delay their sexual maturation for years. . . . The lot of
the male is not always enviable. In one case, *Ceratius,*
the male is absorbed into his wife's body until nothing
remains of him but his sex organs. He has no senses,
no alimentary canal, no independent movement—the
ultimate in subjugation."

Unless all the genetic surgeons of the future are female, it isn't at all likely that man will pattern himself
after *Ceratius.* But it is not inconceivable that he will
want to emulate some of these other creatures. It has
frequently been said that if men could be women and
women men—even for short periods—many of the
conflicts that have simmered and sometimes raged between the two sexes these many centuries might fade
away. At any rate, this sort of "sexual dimorphism"
would unquestionably provide life with a whole new
dimension—and one that might prove highly practical
in the event of wars or other catastrophes that deci-
mate one sex or the other in the new frontiers of outer
space and in other situations where people are isolated
from members of the opposite sex. In the world of the
future, parents may no longer worry about whether
their next child will be a boy or a girl: he may be
both!

Looking into the distant future, during a discussion
on genetic engineering, Dr. Haldane once commented,
"It may be that our remote descendants will be immortal, sessile [attached to the ground, like flowers]
or born talking perfect English." Almost nothing, apparently, is out of the question.

Dr. Lederberg, looking at the *near* future, believes
the hybridization of man and other animals is just
around the corner. Already laboratory technicians
have grafted human chromosomal material onto that

of other animal species. So far these experiments have been limited to isolated tissue cultures but, says Dr. Lederberg, "Before long we are bound to hear of tests of the effect of dosage of the human twenty-first chromosome (for example) on the development of the mouse or gorilla." In this way, he believes, we will finally produce man-animal chimeras of "varying proportions of human, sub-human and hybrid tissue."

A panel of scientists convened by the Rand Corporation recently predicted that such techniques will be used to create humanlike animals ("parahumans") to perform low-grade labor. That there would be a big demand for such creatures—even in these "civilized" times—can hardly be doubted. The writers of a *Time* magazine cover story on "Inefficiency in America" observed that, despite a high rate of unemployment in early 1970, "employers still have trouble finding anyone who will deign to take a position considered boring or menial. Turnover of workers runs high in the Post Office, with disastrous effects upon efficiency, because few Americans will accept jobs that require work at night or on weekends. *Some restaurateurs are hiring the mentally retarded because they are the only people willing to try—and even take some pride in—mopping floors and washing dishes.*"

Genetic engineering, then, may not only be used to enhance intelligence but also to *decrease* it in some cases, to create a willing and even eager labor force to take care of unpleasant but necessary tasks. Dr. Lederberg emphatically does *not* endorse this sort of hybridization. He constantly warns that it may be undertaken, nonetheless, without "an adequate understanding of human values, not to mention vast gaps in human genetics." A number of questions must be answered, he says, before we proceed. "What," he asks, "is the legal, moral or psychiatric identity of an artificial chimera?" And more important, perhaps, "How is it possible for man to demarcate himself from his isolated or scrambled tissues and organs on one side, and from experimental hybrids on another? Pragmatically, the legal privileges of humanity will remain with objects that look enough like men to grip their consciences, and whose nurture does not cost too much. But rather than superficial appearance of face or chromosomes, a more rational criterion of human identity might be the potential for communication within the species, which is the foundation on which the unique glory of man is built."

Another use may be made of hybrids—one far more alarming than that of low-grade labor. It has been suggested that manlike creatures be bred to provide a ready supply of organs for transplanting—organs that would be wholly compatible with the human body. Would the "sacrifice" of such creatures, sharing as they would some of our chromosomes, constitute murder—morally, if not legally? Or might this problem be circumvented—at least to the satisfaction of the majority—by engineering them in such a way that they would not resemble man, at least externally?

More and more questions will arise as we approach an era of "positive eugenics," a program in which genetic engineering and genetic surgery will be used to design the "New Man," perhaps along lines approved by some federal board or commission. As "the trustee of evolution," Sir Julian Huxley's term, man is going to be faced with awesome responsibilities, problems— and temptations. Some worry that man is really not ready for the job. Dr. George Beadle, another Nobel Prize winner, wonders how we will settle on the characteristics of Superman. "The determination of his skin color alone could start a war," he observes, adding that "man knows enough but is not yet wise enough to make man."

Yet, others are convinced that man will proceed anyway. Dr. N. J. Berrill, a Canadian biologist, points out that "Sooner or later, one human society or another will launch out on this adventure, whether the rest of mankind approves or not. If this happens, and a superior race emerges with greater general intelligence and longer lives, how will these people look upon those of us who are lagging behind? One thing is certain: *they,* not we, will be heirs to the future, and they will assume control." In other words, our leaders are likely to eventually feel that they can no more afford to be without positive eugenics than they can be without the hydrogen bomb.

Other dangers loom. Man's growing ability to manipulate life, though it could be used for great good, in eliminating hereditary defects, for example, leaves many scientists far from optimistic. Dr. Salvador Luria of the Massachusetts Institute of Technology, for example, admits that he has a "tremendous fear of the potential dangers that genetic surgery, once it becomes feasible, can create if misapplied." Suppose, he says, that a country—or even some terrorist group—were to create a virus, using techniques already being developed that would sensitize all those exposed to some particular substance. Even though the country or group might also be exposed to the virus they could take precautions to protect themselves against the lethal substance, then threaten to unleash it unless they get what they want.

"Someone," Dr. Luria points out, "could gain a tremendous control over humanity by spreading such a terrible object, thereby holding the power of life and death over a large number of human beings. This is an extreme and horrible example, almost science-fiction matter, but it emphasizes the kind of thing which has been in my mind every time I have thought about the possibility of genetic surgery and engineering."

Fortunately, such concerns are very much on the minds of a number of other scientists working in this field. The younger scientists, in particular, are taking an active interest in the uses to which their discoveries are being put. And they are warning society to be on guard, scorning the dictum that says men of science are not supposed to enter into any sort of concourse with the lay public. Typical of this new breed of scientists are the three brilliant Harvard Medical School researchers who, in late 1969, announced that they had isolated—for the first time ever—a single gene, thus bringing much closer the day when it will be possible to engineer the individual units of heredity.

The three immediately called a press conference, not to gloat over their advancement, which brought acclaim from all corners of the scientific world, but to warn society that their discovery, against their wishes, could be used for evil. "We don't want to work in an ivory tower," said Dr. Jonathan Beckwith, who headed the project. "We don't want to make some contribution to science, then turn it over to the government and say, 'Do whatever you like with this.' Twenty-five years from now we don't want to be a group of J. Robert Oppenheimers [atomic scientists], beating our breasts and mumbling mournfully, 'we shouldn't have done it.' "

Lawrence Eron, a twenty-five-year-old medical student and a member of the Harvard team, added that "We did this work for scientific reasons. But the more we thought about the rapid progress which is taking place in the field of human genetics, the more the consequences of our work conjured up possibilities for both evil and good." He pointed out, for example, that it might be possible "for dictators to use this technique in the distant future to eliminate dissent by injecting genes into humans which would make their behavior more placid, more assenting."

Since speaking out, Dr. Beckwith notes, the group (the third member of which was Dr. James Shapiro) has come in for a good deal of criticism—mostly from older colleagues who "advise us to get out of the field entirely or to keep our mouths shut." But says Dr. Beckwith, "In a free society such as ours, should truths be made available to the people or hidden from them?" Clearly, he and his colleagues feel that it is their duty to let society know what is in the offing, in the hopes that it will act to circumvent the worst and help promote the best.

Again, balance is what is called for. The dangers

must be kept very firmly in mind but not permitted to so outweigh the good that we turn our backs entirely on the great promise of genetic engineering. Tens of thousands of Americans are born every year maimed, retarded and fatally disabled by genetic disorders that could be entirely eliminated by discovery or development of viruses capable of carrying enzymes for repair or modification of genes into the individual cells. This alone is reason enough to pursue genetic engineering and even to institute a crash program—on par with that of the space effort in the 1960s—to seek out and even create such viruses. Now that the means for doing this are at hand it is almost criminal to hesitate.

# THREE

# Cloning: How to Have a Thousand Identical Twins

Before man is deleting unwanted genes with laser erasers and inserting others with viral transducers, he will very probably be manipulating the chromosomal content of DNA in such a way that sex will no longer play any part in reproduction. One technique directed at achieving parthenogenesis, or "virgin birth," has already been applied to plants and animals. Soon it will almost certainly be applied to man. Before long we may hear of a meeting something like the following:

The time: A crisp, clear evening in 1975.

The place: A glass-domed conference room at the U. S. Manned Space Center, Houston.

A dozen leaders of the American space effort, the chairman of select congressional committees and a representative of the Office of the Executive sit facing a lectern at the end of the long, oval table. Everyone is silent, expectant.

Dr. Eric Lehmann, NASA's director of Space Colonization, enters the room, goes to the lectern and reads this statement: "Gentlemen, it is my pleasure to announce that our panel of distinguished geneticists, working with our experts in the field of bioastronautics, have selected from a field of fifty finalists the man whose one hundred clonal offspring will—twenty-five years from today—begin the arduous task of colonizing the moon. The man, a twenty-five-year-old rookie in our training program, has been declared perfect in every respect to serve as the model moonman. This prototype, hereafter known as Mr. X, will be cloned immediately."

Cloning? A put-on—or the latest in science fiction? Actually, it's neither; cloning is strange enough, all right, and, in fact, is probably the most bizarre development to come along in the field of biology to date. But it is also one of the most significant, a scientific breakthrough with mind-stretching implications for the future. Cloning will make it possible for society to reproduce prize bulls, race horses, Olympic-caliber athletes, war heroes, great philosophers, leading scientists, even rock musicians like Ringo Starr by the tens, hundreds or even thousands. And each will be a precise duplicate, a carbon copy of the original.

If one Einstein could lay down the whole foundation of modern-day physics, what might a dozen—or a thousand—Einsteins, either working together or individually, accomplish? Think of the talents of a Mozart or a Beethoven or a Beatle amplified fifty or one hundred times. (Granted, some may find the thought unbearable.) Or imagine the power and discipline of an army whose members are all copies of a Congressional Medal of Honor winner, all united by the same attitudes and objectives and able to communicate with one another with a minimum of words. Apply the same imagination to astronauts, space colonizers, underwater explorers and surgical teams.

Cloning may even have a welcome surprise in store for the "common man," making it possible for him to achieve a sort of immortality; as soon as he dies, his family or friends can simply make a whole new copy of him. Less welcome to some may be the fact that cloning will almost surely take sex out of reproduction, though probably not out of our lives. (Even today sex and reproduction can be separated.) Cloning, in fact, is destined to revolutionize nearly every one of man's traditional notions about how he comes into the world and how nature changes him over the centuries.

As the Nobel Prize-winning geneticist Joshua Lederberg put it, cloning places man "on the brink of a major evolutionary perturbation." And though cloning so far has been achieved only in lower life forms, Dr. Lederberg adds that "there is nothing to suggest any particular difficulty about accomplishing this in mammals or man, though it will rightly be admired as a technical *tour de force* when it is first accomplished."

Like Kimball Atwood, a professor of microbiology at the University of Illinois, he believes this could occur at almost any moment. With a crash program, Dr. Atwood claims, "it could be done now." But even in the normal course of events, he expects it to take place "within a few years."

Cloning (a word which comes from a Greek root meaning "cutting") is generally defined as "asexual propagation," which simply means reproduction without sex or, put another way, reproduction without fertilization.

Cloning makes it possible for a woman to bear a child without the hitherto necessary union of egg and sperm. More incredibly, it will also make possible the birth of a child whose *only* parent is a male. In either case, the clonal offspring will have only one parent and will become the *identical* twin of that parent.

To get a better grasp of this, let's go back to Houston for a minute, where Mr. X was about to give "birth" to centuplets. Listen to the rest of the fictional Dr. Lehmann's speech: "Several thousand body cells will be removed at once," he explains to the assembled dignitaries, "from a tiny patch on Mr. X's forearm. Each cell will be examined for minute chromosomal damage, and the one hundred soundest cells will be retained for implantation into one hundred host cells.

"Nine months from now," he goes on, "one hundred little Mr. Xs will arrive—identical in every detail to their sole parent. For the next twenty-five years a NASA team, headed by Mr. X himself, will train our one hundred-strong clone for the mission to come. Then, one fine day in the year 2000, Mr. X, then fifty years old, will lead the nation in bidding farewell to his one hundred identical sons, if we may call them that, bound for a new life on the moon."

To understand this fantastic state of affairs, it is necessary to review a little basic biology. Remember, first of all, that there are two general kinds of cells: body cells, each of which has a nucleus containing forty-six chromosomes, and sex cells (sperm in the male, ova or eggs in the female), each of which has only half as many chromosomes as the body cells. (That's why you have to get two of them together to make a new individual; half of the chromosomes come from the mother, half from the father.)

The human egg cell is very tiny but is actually not much different from a chicken egg. The yoke, or nucleus, is even the same color as the chicken's yoke. The clear material around the nucleus is called cytoplasm and can be compared to the "white" of the chicken egg. The cytoplasm contributes nothing to the genetic makeup of an individual, since the genes are inside the chromosomes and not the cytoplasm. The job of the cytoplasm is simply to protect and nourish the nucleus and its pay load.

Or so everyone thought until relatively recently when a very important, additional function was revealed: Something in the cytoplasm seems to act as a control center that tells the nucleus when to "switch on," that is, when to start dividing, thus creating new cells and ultimately a new human being. As long as the egg nucleus just sits there with only twenty-three chromosomes, the cytoplasm does nothing. But as soon as the sperm (much tinier than the egg) swims through the cytoplasm and penetrates the nucleus, the cytoplasm is chemically "programed" to send a message to the nucleus which says, in effect, "you are now a fertilized egg cell, complete with forty-six chromosomes, and as such you must start dividing at once." Which is precisely what happens. The "switched-on" cell takes off, dividing billions of times to make a whole new individual.

All of those billions of body cells in any given individual have a common ancestry: the single, fertilized egg cell; they *all* contain an identical set of chromosomes. Yet *unlike* the fertilized egg cell, the body cells have limited and very specialized creative capabilities. Some make only teeth, others form nothing but liver and still others go into making up nothing but hair. And so on. Each body cell has the full number of chromosomes necessary to start an entire new individual, but most of the mechanisms inside them seem to be "switched off." The components in the forty-six chromosomes of a skin cell, for example, are all turned off except for those that go into making skin. So, in a sense, most of the cell is "wasted."

For years, scientists have been fascinated with the idea of taking a body cell and switching it on so that it would start dividing, thus creating a replica of the individual from which it came. No sexual union would be necessary in this sort of reproduction, they reasoned, since all forty-six chromosomes would already be present in the single cell. Incredible as the whole theory seemed, no one could think of any valid objections to it; but neither could anybody think of a way to bring this feat off, even in the lowliest forms of life.

Nobody, that is, until Professor F. C. Steward of Cornell University scored the long-awaited breakthrough a few years ago. His experiments were with nothing more advanced than carrots, but the results electrified the scientific world. Dr. Steward scraped an unfertilized cell from the body of a carrot and placed it in a specially prepared nutrient bath, which contained, among other things, coconut milk. In this solution the cell began dividing as if it thought it had been pollinated. As Dr. Steward puts it, "It was as if the coconut milk had acted like a clutch, putting the cell's idling engine of growth into gear."

From a single body cell, the Cornell team finally got a mature carrot, complete with roots, flowers and seeds.

"We were hardly prepared," Dr. Steward said, "for such dramatic results." Since then many other carrots, tobacco and asparagus plants have been cloned in this fashion.

Now Dr. J. B. Gurdon of Oxford University has devised an ingenious method of duplicating this feat in the animal kingdom. Building on the pioneering work of Dr. R. Briggs and Dr. T. J. King, two American scientists, Dr. Gurdon uses the following technique to achieve asexual reproduction in the African clawed frog: First, he takes an unfertilized egg cell from a frog and destroys its nucleus with ultraviolet radiation. Then he takes a body cell from another frog (often scraping it from such remote spots as the intestinal wall) and removes its nucleus with the help of a microscope and tiny surgical tools. Next he implants the body-cell nucleus into the egg cell, the original nucleus of which had only half as many chromosomes.

In this way the control center in the egg-cell cytoplasm is "tricked" into thinking that fertilization has taken place, because suddenly it notices that there is a full set of chromosomes in its nucleus. So it is that a body-cell nucleus, which previously was nothing more than a tiny speck of intestine, is "turned on" to divide and produce a spanking new tadpole. And, of course, the most striking part of this is that the tadpole grows up to be an identical twin of the body-cell donor. To demonstrate, even to the layman, that the new frog is the "offspring" of the body-cell donor and not the egg-cell donor, Dr. Gurdon uses frogs of clearly distinctive types as the two donors in each case. Invariably, the new frog is the exact image of the body-cell donor, and microscopic studies show that it owes none of its inheritance whatever to the egg-cell donor. The egg-cell cytoplasm is merely the nutrient material it feeds on in its formative stage.

Dr. Gurdon's work seems to define the state of the art at the present time. Research into cloning is going on at universities and research centers throughout the world, and it should not be long until someone somewhere succeeds in cloning a mammal, bringing very much closer the day when man, himself, will be reproduced in this way.

Dr. Kurt Hirschhorn, chief of the Division of Medical Genetics at the Mount Sinai School of Medicine in New York, is one of many scientists who think that cloning will be applied to man—"perhaps much sooner than people think." Without question, though, human cloning is going to be more difficult than the cloning of carrots or toads, partly because human cells are so small and partly because human eggs must be carried in the womb (at least for the present time), not deposited under a rock or dropped into coconut milk in a test tube.

Still, a technique has already been developed to remove egg cells from such mammals as cows, sheep and horses and put them into other animals. This process, which could be very important to human cloning, is being used at the present time by shrewd livestock breeders to improve their herds. They take a prize cow, for example, and wash hundreds of egg cells out of her oviducts with special hormone preparations. These are then implanted into the uteruses of other, poorer quality cows which, after being artificially inseminated as well, carry the fetuses to term, finally giving birth to calves that really belong—genetically—to the prize cow. In this way an exceptional cow can be made to produce hundreds of offspring —instead of the normal seven or eight—in her lifetime. Soon it is expected that this technique will be applied to humans, primarily to permit the barren woman to carry and give birth to a child for the first time. It will also permit the wealthy woman who does not want to undergo the bother of pregnancy to have a fertilized egg cell removed a few days after conception and implanted in another woman, whom she will pay to have the baby for her. (See Chapter Two of Part One, "Embryo Implants: A Startling New Way to Have a Baby.")

The importance of this technique to cloning humans

is this: It offers a way around tthe nutrient-bath problem. To illustrate how the two techniques will work
together, take the case again of Mr. X, the NASA
rookie who was about to be cloned at the beginning of
this chapter. He has been declared the perfect specimen
to serve as a prototype for the one hundred moonmen
the United States wants to send aloft in twenty-five
years. So doctors take one hundred cells from his arm
(such a small quantity that he doesn't even feel the
scratch) and remove their nuclei. In the meantime, they
have also secured one hundred egg cells, the nuclei of
which have been destroyed with tiny beams of radiation
from a laser. (The one hundred egg cells can be
washed out of the same woman or out of one hundred
different women; it makes no difference so long as they
are all good healthy cells. If they are not yet quite mature they can be grown for a time in a nutrient bath or
even incubated, as was demonstrated in an earlier chapter, inside the womb of a rabbit.)

Using microsurgery, the doctors inject the body-
cell nuclei from Mr. X's arm into the one hundred egg-
cell packages (and packages is all they are, since their
contents have been vaporized). Next, using the techniques of embryo implantation, the one hundred newly
constructed cells are implanted into the wombs of one
hundred women. (These do not have to be the same
women who donated the egg cells in the first place;
again, all that is necessary is that they be healthy and
capable of carrying the embryos to term. Where would
NASA find women for the job? Even without pay—and
they would certainly get that—there would probably
be more volunteers than the space agency could use,
such would be the honor of "mothering" future moonmen. Then, too, there would be the attraction of being
among the first women to experience "virgin birth.")

Women, of course, could contribute the body cells
as well as men. In this case all the clonal offspring
would be females. And the same woman who donates
the egg cell and carries the baby to birth could also
contribute the body-cell nucleus, which would consti-

tute total female monopolization of the reproductive process. Almost any combination is possible, but in every case the new individual will always be identical to the body-cell donor and will owe none of his inheritance to the egg-cell donor.

The biggest challenge for those who would achieve human cloning is simply getting the tiny body-cell nucleus into the egg-cell cytoplasm. "But one you get the chromosomes from the body cell in there," says Dr. Hirschhorn, "there's no reason whatever why the damn thing won't grow just like an ordinary fertilized egg cell." With the advent of test-tube pregnancy, of course, clonists will not have to worry about getting the body-cell nuclei into egg-cell packages. Instead, they will simply do as Dr. Steward did with his carrot cells: drop them into a nutrient solution in a test tube. Then, as soon as development begins, the embryos can be transferred to artificial wombs and carried to term completely outside the human body.

But what will we gain from cloning man? For one thing, a number of geneticists have noted that cloning offers a better means of improving the human species than do such schemes as "germinal choice." Germinal choice, the brainchild of Dr. H. J. Muller, winner of the Nobel Prize in medicine, involves the mating of physically and mentally superior men and women in an effort to achieve a sort of superrace. It has received support from a number of eminent scientists over the years. But critics say that it "smacks of the human stud farm" and does not necessarily guarantee consistent improvement.

There are millions of elements in the human genes and these can combine in millions of different and quite unpredictable ways. Geniuses, for example, quite often give birth to children of only average intelligence. In cloning, however, there are no unknown factors; you can see what you are going to get in advance.

So, instead of the sperm and egg banks that Dr. Muller proposed, Dr. Lederberg predicts that the future will see the development of widespread body-cell banks. The late Dr. Jean Rostand, one of the "Immortals" of the French Academy, suggested that even the average man ought to set aside a few body cells (which can be preserved indefinitely in cell-culture solutions) to serve as the ultimate sort of life insurance. In the event of untimely death, these cells could be taken out of storage and grown into an entire new copy of the deceased individual. This process could be continued indefinitely, thus conferring a sort of quasi-immortality on the person in question.

Some scientists fear that the egotists among us will not wait for death before having copies of themselves made. Lord Rothschild, a noted physiologist, warned a gathering of scientists that self-centered fanatics, in the Hitler mold, might set up shop at home—making dozens of replicas of themselves before society could intervene. Dr. Hirschhorn also has warned against do-it-yourself clonists.

To try to forestall such disasters, Lord Rothschild has proposed the establishment of a Commission for Genetical Control to license clonists. But even more unsettling than the idea of a dozen Hitlers or a score of Stalins is one that originated with Dr. Lederberg. For the same reasons that tribalism and racism have flourished for the past several centuries, he says, "clonism and clonishness will prevail" in the future. The ethnocentrism of clones, embracing thousands, even hundreds of thousands of identical individuals, would unquestionably be formidable. What passes for cliquishness today may look pale alongside that engendered by clones. Each clone, of course, would consist of individuals of only one sex, but does not mean that they would necessarily have to mix with members of other clones (of the other sex) in order to reproduce. Female clones could fertilize themselves, and male clones could replicate themselves, using their own body cells, with the aid of the test tube and the artificial womb.

But if the war of the clones can be forestalled (assuming that society lets things get to such a state in the first place), cloning could offer mankind a great deal. Besides making possible unrestricted duplication of prize cattle, race horses and other animals, it opens up a number of new possibilities for man himself—including, in Dr. Lederberg's words, "the free exchange of organ transplants with no concern for graft rejection." "No concern," since the cells of one member of the clone would be identical in every way—and therefore entirely compatible—with those of any other member.

And the neurological similarities of the members of a common clone, Dr. Lederberg notes, could greatly facilitate communication, making astronauts, soldiers, underwater explorers and others who must work together very closely in environments where rapid, intuitive communication is very important, ideal candidates for cloning. It is well known that identical twins are highly "sympathetic," that is, that they usually enjoy extraordinary rapport, able to communicate with one another, sometimes in an almost telepathic matter or, at any rate, with a minimum of words and gestures. This valuable characteristic would almost certainly be intensified even more with the cloning technique.

Then, too, Dr. Lederberg says, this sort of rapport could go a long way toward bridging the "generation gap" that makes contemporary education such a chore. In the world of the future, teachers may only teach their own clonal offspring.

Dr. J. B. S. Haldane, one of the first to propose cloning people, recommended that geniuses and others who make extraordinary contributions to society be cloned. They could use their "retirements," he said, to teach their clonal offspring all they knew. Individuals valued for their physical abilities—dancers, athletes, soldiers, astronauts and so on, he added, should be cloned as young as possible so that they would still have enough vigor left to train their replicas when the time came.

Always practical, Dr. Haldane also proposed that some considerable effort be given to seeking out and cloning individuals with "special effects." Special effects include lack of the pain sense, night vision, resistance to radiation, inability to hear or be affected by high-pitched sounds (the sort which might be used in sophisticated weapons of the future), dwarfism (which might come in handy in the high gravitational fields of some of the other planets we will eventually visit and possibly colonize) and so on.

So even if you don't think you are one of the great thinkers of the twentieth century, take heart; cloning may yet have something for you. As one geneticist puts it, "Who is to say what the future will hold, particularly as we move out into space with its unknown environments. In the year 2000, for example, circumstances might be such that big feet will be in great demand and fat, stubby legs among the most highly valued attributes of the day." And then all size twelves to the fore.

And if you don't have any of the *physical* qualities in demand, you still might make it. Dr. Haldane has observed that "on the general premise that men will make all possible mistakes before choosing the right path, we shall no doubt clone the wrong people. However, everyone selected for this purpose will presumably exceed the median considerably in some respect, if only as a humbug."

# III.

# BRAVER YET...

The great biological discoveries of the recent past promise man more than mere dominion over his body; they offer also to liberate his mind and perhaps ultimately even to free his spirit from the confines of the flesh for all time. As man changes his body, he will change his brain—and his thoughts; indeed, the very way in which man formulates his thoughts, let alone the things he thinks, may be radically altered. He may share his consciousness with a hundred or even a million other men; his brain may become but a single cell in a consciousness of cosmic proportions; perhaps his brain will be linked directly to a computer —either to send commands through it or, more ominously, to receive orders *from it;* possibly his brain will be transplanted from one individual to another; more astounding, he may be able to receive *memory* "transplants," not only from other men but also from animals as diverse as the crocodile and the cougar; perhaps he will live forever and traverse the universe with the agility and speed of light.

All of these possibilities—and they are *that,* despite their science-fiction proportions—are discussed in the following three chapters. The first chapter of this final section, "Molecular Mastery of the Mind: Education by Injection," explores the rapidly developing field of molecular neurology, an off-shoot of the molecular biology that promises to make possible genetic surgery. Here, though, we are concerned with the molecules of the mind, the residing place of knowledge and memory. Until very recently it was believed that these rather ethereal quantities were purely electronic phenomena; now it is known that they have a tangible, *chemical* identity as well; very possibly, say several leading scientists, it will one day be routine to tap them, bottle them and even sell them across the counter. "Quite soon," Jean Rostand once said, "people will buy genius or sanctity at the chemist's just as now women buy the straightness of their nose or the depth of their gaze at the beauty parlor." Already, as we shall see, some tiny animals have geen induced —by man—to "eat" their educations.

The second chapter, "The Scientific Quest for Immortality," is concerned with one of man's most abiding obsessions: longer life. Pacts with the devil used to be the only sure way of achieving immortality, if literature can be trusted, and those always seemed to be far from satisfactory; Satan's conscripts, at any rate, generally ended up asking for their mortality back. The prospects for immortality in the past have been as ephemeral as life itself. Now, with the advent of Participatory Evolution, however, man sees clearly the possibility of programing into his genotype a longer life span, of controlling, at will the subtle, genetic mechanisms of aging. Cryogenics (the "deep-freeze" approach to immortality) induced hibernation and animated suspension, chemical life preservatives, electronic re-energizers, all of these are avenues into a world in which, ironically, death—not life—could become the most sought after luxury.

Chapter Three, "The Cyborg: Evolution to Machine—and Beyond," plots man's course from cybernetic organism to computer being to electromagnetic lattices of pure light. The marriage of man to machine has already been initiated; man has already served as the central nervous system of some very sophisticated new machines; his brain has already been linked directly to a computer and wired with implanted electrodes that cannot only record but also *direct* his activities and emotions. The question now is: Will man evolve into conscious machines or simply be replaced by them? This is not a fanciful question, for as we shall see, computers are very rapidly approaching "states of mind" that many scientists say must be equated with human consciousness.

# ONE

# Molecular Mastery of the Mind: Education by Injection

Who among us has never wondered what another person is thinking about at a particular moment—or what people, and especially famous people, of past eras thought about things? Getting at other people's thoughts is no easy matter. How many times have you offered somebody a penny for his thoughts—and got back a penny's worth of information? How many times have books about the ideas and philosophies of people from the present or the past seemed completely inadequate? If your experience is anything like my own—and, I suspect, just about everybody else's—you'll have to admit that these things happen frequently.

Imagine how much better it would be if there were such things as memory "transplants," simple procedures by which you could tune in—temporarily—on the thoughts of another individual, so that you would actually *share* that person's mind for a time, even if he were long dead. Imagine being able to check in at a "molecular memory bank" or "mind library" where, instead of selecting books from a shelf, you ask for a particular pill, which has a numerical code listed in the card files. You present the number to the "librarian" and when you have the pill, retire to a cubicle. There you down your memory capsule and suddenly find yourself "high" on the thoughts of a great mathematician, musician, philosopher, novelist, humorist, or whoever it is that you have "checked out." Insights into the man's work, his ideas, theories, thoughts flood through you; it is almost as if you *are* that other person. In minutes you know more about him than you could ever know from months or even years of study or reading about him. Gradually, the effect of the "drug" wears off, and you emerge from your cubicle— but you are no longer quite your old self; after all, you have been inside the mind of a great man.

Impossible? No. Not likely to happen tomorrow but far from impossible. And there are other probabilities. Instead of spending months learning a new language —and years if we are to become really proficient at it —we may, in the future, simply submit to an injection of some fluid marked "French" or "Italian" or "Chinese" or whatever language it is we wish to know. And *voila!* Instantaneously we are speaking the lingo with the best of the natives. Or perhaps what we need is an injection of something that will "teach" our brain cells algebra or nuclear physics overnight.

For amusement, we may want to take an injection that will temporarily turn us into tigers, or at least provide us with tigerlike sensations. Or maybe before donning our aqua lung we'll want an injection of some synthetic molecules from the brain of a porpoise. Man-animal "mind trips" like these could make LSD look like child's play.

Less amusing could be the exploitation of mind-control techniques by unscrupulous governments. In the foreseeable future, scientists say, it will be possible for dictators, if they are so inclined, to control the masses by chemically "erasing" unpleasant memories, memories that night reflect unflatteringly on the regime in power, and by inserting other memories— "memories" of things that never happened, "memories," in this case, that would make the regime look good or instill in the governed a loyalty that might be unjustified by the deeds of the government.

You still think all of this is far-fetched? Listen to what Dr. Desmond King-Hele, a distinguished author, futurologist and space scientist at the Royal Aircraft Establishment in Britain, has to say about control of the brain: "The brain is waiting to be understood, too," he writes in *New Scientist,* "and sleep may be one of the liveliest areas of research. In the rat-race of modern urban life, leadership is often decided by staying-power in late-night bargaining. We have government by the sleepless for the sleepy, ritualized in the all-night sittings of the House of Commons. Control of sleep would give more normal sleepers a chance to participate too.

"We may also come to understand the processes of memory and learning. When trained planarian worms are chopped up and fed to untrained specimens, the eaters acquire the skills of the eaten. [More on this important experiment below.] Naive mice can derive similar benefit from being injected with extracts from the brains of trained rats. Shall we too have memories injected? Ten minutes in the treatment room rather than 10 years in the classroom? Drugs to destroy memory, to the delight of every devilish brainwasher? Certainly we may expect to see drugs for curing all mental aberrations, and producing any emotion. The prospect of a pill-powered population is distinctly depressing to most of us. But how could we object to a harmless happiness-drug like the soma of Huxley's *Brave New World?* Some people are permanently cheerful right now: why not everyone?"

Dr. King-Hele goes on to say that "biological prediction is often too timid, and much that I have mentioned could come before the year 2000." In light of the sort of power we can *already* exert over our minds and our moods, this prognostication doesn't seem at all unreasonable. Before launching into an explanation of some of the research that could eventually make possible such things as education by injection, let's consider some of the things available for control of our brains *right now.*

In early 1970, researchers in the psychology department of Princeton University announced that they had isolated and identified a chemical that has the power to switch on and off "the killer instinct" in rats. They said that, by injecting or withholding the chemical, they could turn killer rats into pacifists and peaceful rats into murderers. The discovery was met with considerable excitement, since it indicated that murderous behavior in humans might be subject to similar pharmacological control. It also conjured up the horrifying possibility of turning ordinary, peaceful individuals into mindless killers, demonstrating again that great promise in the biological sciences is almost always accompaned by great peril.

The researchers—Douglas Smith, Melvyn King and Bartley Hoebel—separated their lab animals into two categories: "killers" and "non-killers," prior to any treatment. The killers were those that killed mice placed in their cages in less than two minutes on any three days in a row. Non-killers were those that killed none of the mice, even though they were exposed to them for seventeen days in a row. Then the researchers introduced carbachol into the brains of the non-killers via cannulas that had been implanted prior to the separation procedure. Carbachol is a chemical substance that mimics the behavior of the chemical nerve transmitter acetylcholine. When the substance reached the lateral hypothalamus of the non-killers' brains they *all* turned into killers. When the drug was applied to a portion of the brain only a millimeter (four one-hundredths of an inch) away from the lateral hypothalamus, the non-killers remained peaceful, indicating the precision with which such chemical controls can be wielded.

The researchers also found that they could turn killers into non-killers by applying methyl atropine to the hypothalami of the killer rats. It seems that this chemical blocks the action of naturally occurring acetylcholine, which is normally controlled by an enzyme. This chemical turned the killers into harmless pacifists that sniffed and followed the mice but did nothing to harm them. All of this, the researchers concluded, "raises the practical possibility that pharmacological manipulation of such a system [in man] could be used in the treatment of pathologically aggressive behavior." Recall that in Part Two of this book Dr. Stanfield Rogers observed that "there might be a specific genetic deficiency disease relating to each individual enzyme in the metabolic pathways in the body. . . . all of our diseases . . . even the ubiquitous disease called 'aging,' are genetically conditioned." The Princeton research just discussed indicates that even pathological killing may be something of an enzyme-deficiency disease.

Man, of course, has been dosing himself with sedatives, tranquilizers and stimulants for some time (around fifteen billion of these pills are consumed in the United States alone each year), trying to control his minor hostilities and depressions. Dr. Kenneth Moyer of the Carnegie-Melon University in Pittsburgh believes we are fast approaching the day when governments will act to diminish violence and keep people in line by force-feeding them anti-hostility drugs. "It's not scientifically possible yet to add anti-hostility drugs to the water supply," he notes, "but we're kidding ourselves if we think it's not going to happen."

Total chemical manipulation, much of it for our own good, is predicted by Dr. David Krech in *Saturday Review*. "Both the biochemist and the teacher of the future will combine their skills and insights for the educational and intellectual development of the child. Tommy needs a bit more of an immediate memory stimulator; Jack could do with a chemical attention-span stretcher; Rachel needs anticholinesterase to slow down her mental process; Joan some puromycin —she remembers too many details and gets lost." And so on.

The drugs Dr. Krech mentions are already available. And there are many others. Injections of such things as strychnine, picrotoxin and metrazol—all of which stimulate the central nervous system—make rats learn mazes in less time. So do potassium ions. Calcium ions seem to have the opposite effect, slowing down the learning time. Still other drugs radically alter behavior and mood. There are powerful depressants that can turn happy, well-adjusted people into potential suicides or render them incapable of carrying out simple tasks. The chronoleptogenics distort one's sense of time to the point where the user—one should say "victim"—is no longer able to distinguish between minutes and hours. Euphoriants—not of the sort available on the shelves of drugstores or even by prescription—have been produced that make the user happy, no matter what happens; he would even find a severed arm hilarious, until he bled to death. And there are "disinhibitors" that cause the victim to lose all control over himself so that he talks, walks and generally carries on with wild, exaggerated flourishes. Cataplexogenics, on the other hand, render one's muscles completely inoperable.

"As we stand at the threshold of the chemopsychiatric era and look towards the future," Dr. Robert de Ropp has written, "some may feel disposed to cheer and some to shudder." The mixed bag of drugs listed above goes a long way to explain this mixed reaction. And yet, the sort of control, on the one hand, and liberation, on the other, that can be effected by these chemicals is only a shadow of what is coming, as we learn how to manipulate the molecules that seem to be the repositories of memory. This is the sort of manipulation that could ultimately lead to the "memory bank" that we visited at the opening of this chapter.

In order to understand just how cross-species "mind trips," education by injection, "memories" of things that never happened and so on may come about, it is necessary to take a look at the new science of molecular neurology. Given its name by Dr. Francis O. Schmitt, the Massachusetts Institute of Technology brain researcher, molecular neurology aims to unlock the innermost secrets of the brain. It recognizes that the brain's fantastic capacity cannot be explained in terms of the simplistic electrical theory that held sway for so long. (The incredible capacity of the human brain can perhaps best be demonstrated by pointing out that the magnetic tape of a computer "memory" would have to be several million miles long to rival the memory of a single man.) In place of the old theory, this new science posits an electrochemical model that promises to place man, for the first time, in complete control of his mind and his memory.

The precise nature and locus of memory have been one of the most enduring and entrancing mysteries ever to confront science. Socrates used to spend hours musing over the "character" of memory; so did Shakespeare, who alternately regarded it, depending upon his mood, as a relentless and satanic foe or as a gentle friend, a source of solace and companionship. With the advent of early computers, many of which utilized resonating circuits as memory devices, scientists began to speculate that human memory might be a similar electrical phenomenon. They envisioned "bits" of data in the form of nerve impulses reverberating endlessly around loops made up of the brain's nerve cells, ready to be retrieved whenever needed. The late biologist Sir Charles Sherrington, a strong adherent of this theory, provided its most poetic summation when he compared the brain to "an enchanted loom where millions of flashing shuttles weave a dissolving pattern."

Many scientists, however, were troubled by the theory, pointing out that the brain's ten billion neurons would have to accommodate some remarkably complex interconnections in order to store the estimated million billion bits of information that an individual brain accumulates in a lifetime. Later experiments, moreover, convincingly demonstrated that electronics could not be the sole arbiter of memory. If it were, massive electrical shocks could be expected to "wash out" the tenuous impulses that were said to be bounding endlessly through the brain, leaving the victim totally amnesic. Electroshock experiments with rats and other animals demonstrated that memory of recently acquired knowledge could be obliterated in this way. But once the knowledge had "set" (in many cases within a few minutes of its acquisition), the shock had no effect. The clear implication was that memory is indeed, initially, an electrical phenomenon, but one that quickly translates itself into something less vulnerable and more lasting.

When molecular biology revealed that the blueprint of an entire individual is contained in the microscopic DNA molecule, brain researchers reasoned that memory might also be stored in similar molecules, capable of capturing and encoding the electrical impulses that continually bombard the brain via the five senses. The electrochemical theory of memory was thus born, and it was not long until dramatic evidence began to accumulate in its support, startling researchers around the world, recognizing as they did the awesome eventualities that could accrue as a result of these discoveries.

But what molecules encompass memory? Dr. Holger Hydén of the University of Göteberg in Sweden was the first to provide any sort of answer. In the late 1950s and early 1960s, he conducted a series of intricate experiments with laboratory animals, noting that the RNA content of trained rats was substantially greater than that of their untrained brethren. (RNA is another of the complex nucleic acids and one that works in intimate alliance with the "master molecule" DNA in the control and replication of life.) Dr. Hydén observed that the RNA not only increased with training but changed in chemical composition, as well. That RNA could indeed be the encoder of memory certainly seemed plausible enough since there are at least twenty million RNA molecules in every one of the brain's neurons, easily enough to combine in a million billion different patterns.

Further and more sensational evidence that RNA is a prime mover in the making of memories began to surface when the imaginative Dr. James V. McConnell of the University of Michigan announced that some primitive little worms known as planarians had "eaten their education." The planarians were taught— by means of electroshock—to avoid certain parts of their training mazes. Later they were chopped up and fed to completely untrained planarians. These unschooled cannibals were able to learn the maze, avoiding all the "forbidden" turns, in far fewer trials than other untrained worms fed on less brotherly fare.

Though such experiments immediately conjure up the specter of cannibalism in the classroom, there is little likelihood of *human* pupils ever getting an education in this way. Planarians were apparently able to absorb the RNA of their departed peers directly into their mini-brains from their digestive tracts. Higher species will require a more sophisticated approach.

A step in that direction has already been taken by Dr. Allan L. Jacobson and his colleagues at the University of California at Los Angeles. Originally one of Dr. McConnell's associates, Dr. Jacobson struck off on his own and began experimenting with rats and hamsters. He taught the animals to perform specific skills, killed them and extracted RNA from their brains. This heady brew was injected into untrained animals, which then acquired the skills in question with uncommon speed. The UCLA team, moreover, discovered that memories could cross the so-called "species barrier." Rats, that is, were able to acquire new skills from the RNA of hamsters and vice versa.

In a similar series of experiments, Dr. Georges Ungar of the Baylor University College of Medicine, taught Swiss mice to ignore loud noises that would normally make them cringe in fear, then sacrificed them and injected proteinlike molecules from their brains into unconditioned mice. Thus treated, the untrained mice were completely unmindful of loud noises. As for the difference in molecules here, it is now suspected that certain proteins may actually be the final resting place of memory, but both the quantity and quality of the protein molecules are, in any event, determined by the instruction-laden RNA molecules, preserving for the latter a critical, central role in memory "manufacture."

All of these "transplant" experiments touched off a storm of controversy within the scientific community, and a number of researchers questioned their veracity. Now, however, one of the most prominent of the original "doubters," Dr. William L. Byrne of Duke University (working with Dr. David Samuel of Israel's famed Weizmann Institute), has achieved a successful memory transplant of his own. Dr. Byrne now flatly declares that "memory transfer is a real phenomenon."

So, also, it appears, is "memory erasure," a technique, as was noted earlier, that could be used for great evil as well as for great good. A leading light in this field is Dr. Bernard W. Agranoff of Michigan University's Mental Health Research Institute. He found that a certain antibiotic called puromycin halts the synthesis of protein molecules, apparently by inhibiting the normal functioning of RNA. Dr. Agranoff trained goldfish to ring bells in order to obtain their food, then injected puromycin into their brains, causing them to forget entirely this intensively conditioned skill.

It is hoped that more refined drugs, patterned after this one, might eventually be used to selectively blot out the crippling memories of many neurotics and psychotics, allowing them to resume useful lives. It has also been suggested that such drugs might be used by political powers to literally brainwash enemies or rebellious subjects, making them "forget" the atrocities of their leaders. When asked by a reporter whether the Central Intelligence Agency had an interest in his work, Dr. Agranoff smilingly replied, "I forget."

Though researchers have had to proceed with extreme caution, memory experiments have already been conducted with man. So far both their intent and their consequences have been benign. Operating on the premise that an increased availability of RNA ought to enhance memory, Dr. D. Ewen Cameron of the Veterans Administration Hospital in Albany, New York, has administered RNA extracted from yeast to elderly patients plagued by forgetfulness. Crude as this approach was, he reported that many of the patients exhibited improved alertness and memory during treatment. He found, however, that the improvement faded quickly when treatment ceased.

Subsequently, Abbott Laboratories of Chicago discovered a chemical compound known as magnesium pemoline, or Cylert. Though its developers have resisted hailing it the long-awaited "memory pill," others have been less cautious. Results, in any event, have been encouraging. Cylert works by stimulating a brain enzyme that plays an important role in the production of RNA. Cylert-treated rats learned given skills faster and remembered them far longer than untreated rats, encouraging Dr. Cameron to try the new drug on his forgetful patients. Early findings indicate that Cylert works as well on humans as it does on rats. Some patients who could not even remember how to turn on their television sets have regained this vital ability, thanks to Cylert. Others who found it difficult to recall the procedure for tying their shoes have returned to the bridge table.

Ultimately, it is believed, specific memories (which for most practical purposes constitute what we call "knowledge") will be readily available in the form of pills or injections possibly containing benign viruses capable of penetrating the blood-brain barrier and "infecting" the brain cells with the desired information. Viruses are ideal for these molecular-mind missions since many of them are nothing but cores of protein-coated RNA anyway. In addition, they are probably the only agents capable of getting inside the desired cells at the desired time. Just as the molecular biologists are certain that genetic surgery is imminent, so the molecular neurologists are confident that the practicality of made-to-order, synthetic memories are just a matter of time.

When that times comes, attaining fluency in French

or whatever other language you prefer will, quite literally, be no more painful than a polio vaccination. This will be just as true for algebra, organic chemistry, musicology, law and perhaps even tennis. Dr. Krech, a professor of psychology, active in memory research at the University of California at Berkeley, has coined the tongue-twisting word "psychoneurobiochemeducation" to describe this merging of psychology, brain chemistry and education.

Two French researchers, Drs. Alexandre Monnier and Paul Laget, have gone so far as to suggest that in the world of tomorrow, we may not have to learn anything, even by injection. Instead, they predict, we will be *born* with a full set of "memories" bred into us via genetic engineering. This is what the late Dr. J. B. S. Haldane had in mind when he said that our children may one day come into the world "speaking perfect English."

Though most of the research to date has involved rats and other laboratory animals, it should be amply clear that the ultimate target of all this new knowledge is man himself. It is not difficult to envision some of the blessings—and some of the horrors—that memory manipulation could visit upon mankind. We have already seen how memory deletion or erasure could be used to free individuals from the bonds of unhappy memories. And on the other hand we have also seen how similar techniques could be used to effect a unique sort of cosmetic surgery of the mind, for the purpose of excising memories of a subject population that might otherwise undermine confidence in the Establishment that holds power. In addition, agents such as puromycin could give bacteriological warfare a new dimension, destroying memories and thus, presumably, the will to resist a take-over, as well.

Memory insertion may also have its sinister side. Totalitarians could conceivably use memory manipulation to achieve the ultimate propaganda mechanism, controlling loyalties, attitudes and prejudices, instilling hopes and fears. People could easily be "programed" to remember things that never happened and forget things that did.

Even leaving dictators and brainwashers out of it, memory manipulation could have some unpleasant—and *complicated*—effects on society. To illustrate, let's plunge into a futuristic soap opera set, say, in the year 2000. Let us start out with the improbable and assume that marriage is still a going concern in that year and that (much less improbably) memory transplants have been perfected. Our leading characters are Mr. Jones and Mr. Smith. Mr. Jones is brilliant, handsome, successful, a leader in the community. Mr. Smith is less brilliant, not at all handsome, far from successful and anything but a leader. But he *does* have a beautiful wife.

As happens in soap operas, Mrs. Smith falls in love with Mr. Jones and vice versa. They have a torrid affair. Mr. Smith catches them *flagrante delicto* and sinks into black depression. He broods and broods over what to do; he wants to kill himself but hesitates, knowing that this is exactly what Mr. Jones and Mrs. Smith want him to do. Mr. Smith is dumb but he's not stupid; he knows that his life for all intents and purposes is over (he loved his wife, you see), but he is not going to give it up without first making sure that the two adulterers pay—and pay and pay.

With the help of *Mrs.* Jones (an acid-tongued harridan addicted to gin), Mr. Smith gets at the brain RNA Mr. Jones has had extracted and set aside as a sort of "insurance" to be used in the event that some accident causes him to lose his memory or part of it. (It is also his secret hope that, since he is an increasingly important man, some of the memory libraries setting up across the country will eventually want to make synthetic copies of his RNA molecules so that everyone can tune in on his mind.) Mrs. Jones assures Mr. Smith that this is the only supply of Mr. Jones's memory molecules available anywhere.

Mr. Smith begins to brighten up. He now has the perfect plan; both revenge and oblivion are within reach. One night after Mr. Jones and Mrs. Smith part company at a motel on the edge of town, Mr. Smith goes into action. He follows Mr. Jones's car down a deserted road, then forces him to the curb with his own car. A bullet wipes the expression of anger off Mr. Jones's face. In another minute, Mr. Smith has set fire to both car and corpse. Then he races back home, arriving there ahead of his wife (who stopped for cigarettes and the evening paper). He aspirates Mr. Jones's brain RNA into a syringe along with another chemical (obtained, again, with the help of the wealthy Mrs. Jones) that will make the "transplant" that is about to take place *permanent*, while completely wiping out his *own* memory. Taking one last look at himself in the mirror, Mr. Smith smiles sardonically, shoots the heady brew into a vein in his forearm and collapses to the floor.

"George!" Mrs. Smith exclaims as she stumbles onto the apparently inert form of her husband a few minutes later. She is about to rush to the telephone to give Mr. Jones the good news when the "body" stirs. Within a few minutes the nightmare unfolds. Not only does Mrs. Smith have to adjust to the notion that the body of her husband is now in possession, for all practical purposes, of the mind of her lover, but her lover (I said these things could get complicated) must now adjust to the fact that he is trapped inside the body of the very man he cuckolded. Only Mrs. Jones sees the justice of it all.

And there's an epilogue, of course. Mr. Jones's charred bones are quickly identified, and the coroner is called in to rule on the nature of the crime that has taken place. After only a moment's study, which takes into account the memory transplant, the coroner (who by this time has seen everything) says the only crime committed was suicide—Mr. Smith's. What do they do for a body at Mr. Smith's funeral? They use what is left of Mr. Jones's body, of course. Curtain.

On the more positive side, memory control promises to revolutionize education, making it possible, as we have seen, to "learn" complex languages and sciences overnight, while simultaneously improving the durability of memory. In addition, it promises to provide a means of perserving the memories—the minds, in effect—of great savants, rendering them, in a sense, immortal. And if memories reside in molecules, as the evidence strongly suggests, then molecular memory libraries are probably inevitable. Instead of books, these libraries will house synthetic copies of brain molecules extracted from leading men of arts and sciences. (The "originals" will be retained in vaults, hopefully better guarded than the one in which Mr. Jones placed his trust.)

The scholar who then wishes to "tune in" on the thinking of a leader in his field will simply go to the library and receive the appropriate injection. Even families may have their own personal "memory banks," which certainly ought to prove more rewarding than family scrapbooks.

Finally, memory control could open up a whole new spectrum of experiences for mankind, perhaps greatly broadening in the process man's understanding of himself and the world around him. Dr. Jacobson has already demonstrated that memories can be transferred from one species to another. This is not surprising on second glance. DNA, after all, is common to *all* life on earth; there is little reason to suspect that the mind molecules would follow a different pattern and be diversified in any radical way among the different species. It is almost certain that one man will eventually be able to acquire the memory, knowledge and mind of another man or woman (this could supplant sex as the ultimate in sharing experiences). It now appears that a man may also be able to acquire the memories and knowledge of *animals*—on a temporary basis, of course. The thrill of prowling a jungle with the instincts of a leopard or of swimming the oceans with the cunning and lore of a dolphin should surely surpass the most profound hallucinogenic "trip." When one speaks of "acid" in the future, one may well be referring to *nucleic* acid.

Where does this leave society? Fortunately, at least a few scientists are beginning to alert the public to the peril of these new manipulative powers. Many scientists, of course, would still prefer to be left alone so that their research can lead them—and *us*—where it will. Dr. Krech, however, is one of those who feel quite differently. Senator Walter F. Mondale (D.-Minnesota) has proposed that a new national commission be established to study the social implications of advances in the health sciences. During Senate hearings on the proposed commission, Dr. Krech summed up the gravity of current brain research which, he said, "is immeasurably more significant for the future of man than anything else now going on in science. It is my judgment that within five to ten years there will be available a regimen combining psychological and chemical measures which will permit us to exercise a significant degree of control over the development of man's intellectual capabilities."

When we are able to manipulate the mind at will in the ways that have been discussed in this chapter, Dr. Krech asks, "Who is to decide what happens to whom? The brain researcher has neither the wisdom nor experience nor knowledge to tell society: 'Don't worry your unscientific heads about all this: *I* will save society —from *me!*' All of society must provide the experts with political and moral and ethical guidance."

## TWO

# The Scientific Quest for Immortality

"Aging and death are not inevitable," says Desmond King-Hele, the British scientist quoted in the last chapter. "Death is merely a convenient evolutionary invention, to clear away creatures that cannot improve and make room for new generations. Aging, being so gradual, presumably depends on very minor biochemical changes, which, once known, may be treatable. An 'immortality pill' would create problems graver than those it solves—a population exploding at 4 per cent per annum, big shots who refuse to retire, and so on."

Yet, despite the dangers, on every scientific frontier —be it physics, chemistry, physiology, genetics, electronics or biology—impressive and sometimes bizarre research is being carried out in strenuous pursuit of immortality. The will not only to live but to live endlessly today galvanizes segments of the scientific community that once exhibited nothing but contempt for the "fictionalists" of life everlasting.

It is estimated that the National Institutes of Health are now spending nearly $50 million annually on hundreds of research projects directly concerned with death and aging. In the United States alone there are some 1500 research teams whose mission can only be described as all-out war against death.

Optimism about the prospects for decisively overcoming the world's number-one killer "disease"—aging—is running high. Dr. A. L. D'Abreu told a gathering of members of the Royal College of Surgeons that even those present might be able to live to be 180, thanks to the massive research effort now underway in nearly all areas of science and medicine. Before looking into various aspects of that effort, let us consider the process of aging itself.

In some respects we begin to decline in energy and mental acuity at the moment of birth, for, by definition, with each passing moment we age, "progressing" inexorably toward death. The real damage, however, begins to set in during the mid-twenties. "You don't feel it right away," one biologist says sardonically, "but by the time you reach thirty your irreplaceable brain cells are already dying off at the rate of about 100,000 every day." Indeed, between the ages of thirty and ninety, provided one lives that long, brain weight drops from an average of more than three pounds to little more than two pounds. Muscle weight falls off by 30 per cent, and with that fall the heart diminishes in efficiency, pumping only half the blood that it did at its peak. The number of nerve fibers in the body falls by a quarter, and those that remain operate 15 per cent more slowly than they once did, substantially dulling our reaction time. Nephrons that remove waste materials from the blood diminish radically, and even our taste buds fall from 250 per papilla in youth to 80 in old age.

What is the mechanism responsible for this ugly decay? Can it be destroyed—or at least thwarted?

A number of theories have been advanced over the years to explain death and aging, but the one that now seems most viable is the so-called cell-death theory. It maintains that senescence sets in due to the random failure and death of cells throughout the body. When enough cells die the entire individual dies. Particularly affected by this process are those tissues that are unable to replace dead cells, namely muscles and nerves.

The fact that so many people die of heart failure (as opposed, say, to liver failure) supports this theory. The heart, unlike the liver, is really just a specialized muscle, the cells of which can never be replaced once destroyed. The liver, on the other hand, can regenerate lost cells in old age just as easily as in youth.

But the question remains: *Why* do these cells die? No one is yet absolutely certain. When we know we will be able to decisively control aging and probably eliminate death—if we wish. A number of theories are presently being discounted. The notions that cells simply "run out of gas," become clogged with their own wastes or are damaged by atmospheric radiation have not fared well under close scrutiny. But a theory proposed by a Finnish chemist, John Bjorksten, has.

Dr. Bjorksten's "cross-linking" theory holds that the long-chain molecules (RNA and DNA) that form the all-important nuclei of the cells slowly become snarled up and thus are unable to function, resulting ultimately in cell death. Dr. Bjorksten—and now many other scientists—believe that stray proteinlike molecules or bits of molecules drift into the cells and accidentally attach themselves at various points to the long-chain molecules. Gradually everything becomes so gummed up that the cell dies. The villains in this case—these stray bits of molecules, the presence of which has been detected chemically and even microscopically—are now known as "age pigments."

Dr. Bjorksten believes there are bacteria that can dissolve these pigments and thus not only delay aging but perhaps arrest cell death altogether. Scientists do have leads that point to the existence of such bacteria, though they have not yet actually isolated them. But even if such bacteria are never found or controlled, it is likely that modern science will one day be able to synthesize agents capable of selectively dissolving the pigments.

The cell-death theory, while it may be adequate to explain normal aging processes, cannot, however, account for the phenomenon we call "overnight aging."

Some creatures, such as the salmon, appear to be naturally "programed" to die what seems to us to be a premature death. When man turns gray "before his time," however, it would appear to be the result of some defect in a still mysterious cellular mechanism. Eventually, scientists are confident this life-span mechanism will be understood and subjected to manipulation. The technology for such feats is, as we have seen in previous chapters, already being perfected by geneticists who are rapidly mastering the science of cellular surgery.

While geneticists learn how to make radical—and lasting—changes in the aging mechanism at the molecular level of life, other scientists are exploring different avenues with considerable promise of success. What follows is a sampling of some of the various approaches:

*Fasting for Immortality?*—Not at all out of the question, say gerontologists, who for years have been pondering the now-famous experiments of Dr. C. M. McCay at Cornell University. Dr. McCay took two groups of rats, all of the same age, and placed them on different diets. One group was fed on a regimen that, while not excessive, insured a maximum growth rate. The other group was given a skimpy bill of fare guaranteed to minimize growth rate. Astoundingly, the "underprivileged" rats lived twice as long as their well-fed brethren. This approach has been followed up by a Chicago research team, which was able to extend the lives of rats by 20 per cent simply by forcing them to fast every third day. One of these researchers was so impressed that he began fasting himself. It seems likely that long-range experiments along these lines will be initiated—using humans—before very long.

Dr. Bjorksten theorizes that fasting prolongs life because it diminishes the consumption of age-pigment molecules that interfere with normal cell functioning. Others believe that fasting simply delays maturation and extends life in the pre-adult period only. This seems to have been the case, at any rate, with Dr. Mc-

Cay's rats. Still, some might argue, it is surely better to add twenty or thirty years to one's life while young rather than when too old to enjoy them.

*Peter Pan Is Alive and Well—in a Hormone*—It was British physiologist Sir Vincent Wigglesworth who discovered him there. Wigglesworth, experimenting with butterflies and other insects that metamorphose from larval to adult stages of development, found that a specific hormone governs this remarkable phenomenon and keeps the insect young until a pre-programed time. Excited cosmetics manufacturers immediately dubbed the chemical in question—which Wigglesworth named "ecdysone"—the "Peter Pan hormone" because it seemed to have the power to keep an organism in a state of androgenous youth, reminiscent of the imperishable Pan.

And, in fact, Wigglesworth did demonstrate that ecdysone could do just that and more—at least in insects. He located the glands that secrete the hormone in a very young insect and transplanted them into a second, older insect that was about to undergo metamorphosis. He was overjoyed to find that the second insect remained a larva and *continued to grow*. When it did at last metamorphose, it was a giant insect. Here was a superior animal, indeed—one that not only lived much longer than its peers but one that also towered over them in physical stature. (And Wigglesworth could have gone on implanting immature ecdysone glands into his experimental animal indefinitely, thus insuring it youthful immortality—and ever-increasing size!)

Could this incredible technique ever be applied to man? Many scientists think so, provided that the human equivalent of ecdysone can be found and isolated. Researchers are encouraged by the fact that cessation of growth and the simultaneous onset of maturity in man are definitely controlled by the brain—and presumably, therefore, by a specific hormone or other chemical. Certainly the prospect of prolonging life at a period when both physical and mental development are approaching a peak is well worth pursuing. The "spin off" of this particular approach to immortality could prove to be nothing less than the emergence of a superrace.

There are other hormones already available which, contrary to what Wordsworth said in his ode on "Intimations of Immortality," *can* bring back "the hour of splendor in the grass and glory in the flower." At least temporarily. Injections of synthetic hormones called "anabolics," for example, can give a seventy-year-old man the muscular strength and tone of a man twenty or thirty years younger, build up his weight, stop bone decay and tighten up the skin. Eventually, it is believed, it may be possible to implant the glands that secrete hormones such as these directly into the aging body, thus circumventing the need for frequent injections.

*The Electronic Pause That Refreshes*—Dr. R. A. Dufee and Dr. R. H. Koontz of Battelle Memorial Institute have performed a startling demonstration suggesting that the presence of negatively charged molecules of air (called ions) in the atmosphere can induce youthful vigor and improve mental acuity in animals. The Battelle team used two groups of laboratory rats. Half the rats were young, only three months old. The other half were fourteen months, retired and well past their prime. Some of the rats—from both age brackets—were housed in a chamber containing normal air (which has about 600 negative ions per cubic centimeter). Another group, also consisting of both young and old rats, was placed in an environment with a concentration of 140,000 negative ions per cc.

It was casually noted some years ago that negative ions seem to have an exhilarating effect on animals, including man, so Drs. Dufee and Koontz were interested in determining the specific effects of a heavy dose of these ions on the performance of animals. For this purpose they used a water maze through which the rats had to wend their way in order to reach a warm, comfortable box. The water was very cold, so the rats had sufficient incentive not to dawdle.

Young rats from the normal atmosphere were able to get through the maze, as expected, much faster than their fathers, who had also been breathing normal air. The *old* rats that had been inhaling air laced with negative ions, however, were able to far surpass the performance of the untreated older rats. The old, ionized rats were able to swim through the maze in only eleven minutes, forty seconds, on the average, compared with a slothful forty minutes, fifty-six seconds, as the average time for the untreated graybeards, who seemed to be confused by the maze. By the second heat, the old, ion-exposed rats were racing through the maze even faster than the untreated young rats!

It seems apparent that negative ions have some definite beneficial effects on the mental and physical performances of aging animals. And since the aging processes in man and other animals do not appear to differ radically, scientists expect that man may also reap the benefits of charged air. Experiments with humans are now being planned.

*It Preserves Potato Chips—So Why Not People, Too?*—"It," in this case, is BHT, a modern chemical additive used to preserve potato chips, salad oils, breakfast cereals and many other foods that sit on the shelves of grocery stores for days, weeks and sometimes even months without spoilage. It took Dr. Denham Harman of the University of Nebraska Medical School to ask, "Why not people, too?" But like all good scientists, Dr. Harman has set to work experimenting with lab animals first. So far the results have been astonishing. Working with two sets of mice—both of the same breed and average age—Dr. Harman found that the animals whose diets included BHT *lived 50 per cent longer* than the mice fed on a diet completely free of BHT. The additive, Dr. Harman believes, slows down the chemical reactions within the body—very possibly at the cellular level—and thus retards aging. More, of course, will have to be known about this seemingly miraculous substance before humans can start taking it on a daily basis (in doses that would far exceed what one normally gets in packaged foods). But its promise is apparent.

*Freeze Now, Live Later*—Cryogenics, the science of super-cool, provides a possible approach to immortality already seized upon by Dr. James H. Bedford. Dr. Bedford, a professor of psychology, died of cancer at age seventy-three. Under the direction of the Cryonics Society of California, his body was immediately injected with heparin, an anticoagulant, and connected to a heart-lung machine. While the heart machine kept blood surging to the brain, the attending physician packed the body in ice, bringing its temperature down to 8 degrees Centigrade.

At this point, the blood was drained from Dr. Bedford's body and replaced with the controversial new wonder drug DMSO—to help keep the cells from bursting under the force of freezing. The body, then packed in dry ice and lowered to a frigid minus-79 degrees C., was flown to the Cryo-Care Equipment Corporation in Phoenix, Arizona, for permanent storage in liquid nitrogen at a temperature of minus-190 degrees C.

Dr. Bedford was neither fanatic nor cultist. Nor did he imagine that the cryo-burial just described would not, in addition to preserving his body indefinitely, do some damage to it. But he hoped that science would, in the decades to come, discover some means of reviving long-frozen bodies and with the technological advances of a new era repair the damage *and* overwhelm whatever disease or trauma had caused death. Dr. Bedford left a legacy of $200,000 to found the Bedford Foundation for Cryobiological Research, whose mission will be to seek ever better methods of storing bodies and then—when science has found a cure for such things as cancer—of reviving them for new life.

Organizations patterned after the Life Extension Society, founded by the physicist Robert C. W. Ettinger, claim thousands of members, dozens of whom have already made arrangements for cryo-burial and for the maintenance of their frozen bodies through the decades to come. There are some eccentrics in the ranks, such as the Oklahoma couple who requested that their pet Chihuahua be frozen and stored with them. There are also some real pioneers, such as the young Frenchman who has volunteered to be frozen right now, without waiting for death by disease, accident or old age. Generally, though, members tend to be well-educated, articulate, prosperous (as one would have to be), and in most cases either atheistic or at least agnostic. None seems worried about the locus of the soul while the body is in suspension.

Dr. Ettinger and his followers are placing all of their faith in medical science, some of whose leaders now predict the successful cold-storage of entire organs as early as 1971. If this is achieved, there is no question that cryogenics will offer a viable approach to dramatic life extension. Insect larvae have been frozen for as long as ten years and then successfully revived. And even dogs and monkeys have "come back from the dead" after being kept at subzero body temperatures for as long as an hour. In an even more promising experiment, Japanese researchers stored the brain of a cat in protective glycerol at minus-20 degrees C. for no less than seven months. They were then able to thaw it out and report that the brain exhibited regular electrical activity.

*Hibernation as a Way of Life*—Or, more to the point, as a way of achieving longer life. Some scientists suggest that long before the deep freeze really proves itself it will become commonplace for man to hibernate like the hedgehog or the bear, thus adding years to his life. Hibernation, after all, is already part of nature's repertoire; a variety of animals do it all the time. Scientists involved in the space effort have been among those particularly keen on adding this phenomenon to man's own bag of tricks. Some have proposed that astronauts hibernate on the long journeys to the outer planets of our solar system and on the even longer forays to the other stars. Hibernation, they argue, would retard aging, minimize the amount of food, water and oxygen required by the astronauts and eliminate the potentially serious problem of boredom on the long journey.

During hibernation, body temperature falls in many cases to only a few degrees above freezing. The lungs draw air only once every two or three minutes. The metabolic rate declines significantly. And the heart, which generally beats about seventy times a minute, slows to five or six strokes per minute, consequently wearing out much more slowly.

Dr. R. J. Chaffee, a zoologist at the University of Missouri, has been conducting research with hamsters that provides some hope that man may eventually be able to reap the benefits of hibernation for himself. Dr. Chaffee worked with two hamster populations— one a hibernating variety, the other a variety that never hibernated. Through interbreeding of the two varieties, he was able to induce hibernation into the stock of the non-hibernating type, proving in the process that the phenomenon is determined by the genetic code. It may, therefore, be possible to discover the enzymes that control this part of the code and inject them, either in natural or synthetic form, into our bodies, inducing hibernation at the desired moment.

In his book *Profiles of the Future,* astrophysicist Arthur C. Clarke predicted that man would achieve suspended animation by the year 2050. Now he has revised his estimate, foreseeing its use in space travel during the first decade of the next century.

Beyond these approaches to immortality, of course, there are a great many others bound to have considerable impact. The heart-lung machine, along with intravenous feeding techniques, for example, have already contributed to the overthrow of our old notions about death. Modern medical technology can keep bodies, if not always minds, functioning for weeks and even years beyond the point that only a short while ago would have been termed clinical death.

Even more dramatic—at least in potential—is the sort of technique developed by Dr. Robert J. White to sustain the life functions of brains *outside* the body. Even at this early stage of research, isolated animal brains and entire severed heads have been kept alive for days. And says Dr. White, "The possibility of maintaining a human brain is definitely there." The "social implications" of such a feat have so far prevented anyone from attempting to sustain a human brain in isolation. But, says Dr. White, "The idea won't seem so overwhelming" in another twenty or thirty years.

Such experiments open up the possibility of maintaining the brain long after the body has become useless—because of accident or disease, extending life in that way. To many, this is certainly a frightening prospect. "It is right," notes *New Scientist,* "that we should pause and consider the long-term implications of the notable technical achievement that Dr. White reports. What dreams may come to a disembodied brain, and what pain, that the mute organ is unable to express? How far along this road does consciousness and individuality persist, and at what point is the owner of the brain deemed to be dead? . . . Where, between the present experiments and the long-range possibility of attempts to preserve an active human mind in a bottle, should we say, 'Stop'? We must remember, too, that here is only one more instance of a remarkable flowering of techniques of many kinds, ranging from prosthetics to chromosomal manipulations, which have tremendous potential for good, but also allow a mockery of nature."

Of course, it may be possible eventually to link these disembodied brains to computers and other devices that would double for the missing body, permitting the brain to communicate and even direct action. This is an era of transplants—though it is an era that is just dawning—transplants not only of natural parts but also of artificial parts. Whereas a new human heart might help an old man live twenty years longer, a plastic heart might enable him to live fifty years beyond the span allotted him by nature, particularly if supplemented with a few of the other mechanical "spare parts" now in the laboratory works. Eventually, some scientists and engineers believe, man may achieve immortality simply by trading in all of his temporal bits and pieces for durable plastic and metal replacements.

Will society be able to cope with all this? In order to grasp the immense complexities posed by immortality, one need only consider the implications of a single approach to it—suspended animation, for example. When a person is deposited in a cryocrypt (of the sort that presently exist in Arizona and California) or a hibernaculum, what rights do his heirs have to his estate? If he is potentially revivable, perhaps they would have no rights? Might they not be tempted, as "caretakers" of his estate, to simply "forget" to revive him when science finally finds a cure for whatever it was that "killed" him?

Could a wife remarry while her husband was in suspension? How will children respond to a suddenly revived father—*who is now younger than they are?* What if the suspendee runs out of maintenance funds; do you then discard his body? Would this constitute murder? Can heirs collect insurance at the time of a man's death, even if that man has opted to go into suspension, while awaiting a cure? More important, what happens to our concept of murder if corpses are potentially revivable? What of suicide? Could a doctor be accused of murder for failure to freeze somebody, or otherwise put them into suspension? What does society do if masses of people, bored with the present-day world, decide to freeze themselves for a century or so, hoping something interesting will be happening when they "come back"?

Then there is the more general—and more pressing—question of world overpopulation. Will only select individuals be crowned with immortality or will the mantle be extended to all? Will society decide to forcibly halt all propagation and simply carry on with those already present and accounted for, engineering evolutionary changes in this perpetual population as environmental requirements change over the centuries? Will man be able to endure the strain of living forever? Will the most valuable members of society be denied the right to die? Will death ultimately become the most sought-after luxury?

# THREE

# The Cyborg: Evolution to Machine— and Beyond

The cyborg—an evolutionary chimera one step in advance of man—is already at large in the land. In a laboratory on the banks of the Hudson River, he communicates flesh-and-blood perceptions through a computer, to which he is linked, without words or even rudimentary gestures; at another laboratory—this one in England—he stops and starts complex machines simply by "willing" them into action or inaction; at a neuropsychiatric institute in San Francisco and a research center in southern California he instantaneously projects his emotions into a motion-picture screen via a meaningful matrix of coded colors and, utilizing this cerebral drama, learns to exercise complete command over his state of mind.

Still other cyborgs—once ordinary human beings— kill whatever they look at with the mere flick of an eye or with the same minute exertion bring an automobile to a grinding halt. Some cyborgs are so "wired" that they can relive past experiences with such vividness that they are unable to distinguish the synthetic experience from the real; others are able to evoke in their own bodies—at will and at a moment's notice— pleasure so profound and all-pervasive that it surpasses anything known to ordinary man.

The cyborg is neither man nor machine but a felicitous combination of the two: a cybernetic organism, a man-machine symbiote functioning harmoniously to create a new individual and perhaps, in the process, a whole new order of life. The cyborg, embracing the revolutionary concept of Participatory Evolution, may do more to change man and his world than anything previously imagined. Even the gene tinkerers, limited as they are to the world of the flesh, may have to take a back seat to the medical engineers and biocyberneticists who are beginning to wed man with machine in an effort to extend, amplify and accentuate his strengths while obliterating his weaknesses.

The possibilities are nothing less than stunning, as suggested by this passage from the conclusion of Arthur C. Clarke's *Profiles of the Future:* "I suppose one could call a man in an iron lung a cyborg, but the concept has far wider implications than that. One day we may be able to enter into temporary unions with any sufficiently sophisticated machines, thus being able not merely to control but to *become* a spaceship or a submarine or a TV network. This would give far more than purely intellectual satisfaction; the thrill that may be obtained from driving a racing car or flying an airplane may be only a pale ghost of the excitement our great-grandchildren many know, when the individual human consciousness is free to roam at will from machine to machine, through all the reaches of sea and sky and space."

Space, more than anything else, fostered the cyborg concept, as first articulated by Dr. Manfred Clynes and Dr. Nathan Kline of Rockland State Hospital in New York. Speaking before the Psychophysiological Aspects of Space Flight Symposium in San Antonio in 1960, they noted that "in the past the altering of bodily functions to suit different environments was accomplished through evolution. From now on, at least in some degree," they continued, "this can be achieved without alteration of heredity by suitable biochemical, physiological and electronic modification of man's existing *modus vivendi*."

Instead of lugging along into outer space extensive and encumbering artificial environments compatible with the present model of man, the two doctors proposed, why not *change* man so that he would himself be compatible with the new environment? The astronautic cyborg they envisioned would be considerably more agile and certainly far more effective than our present-day moonmen. For one thing, the cyborg's spacesuit would be lightweight and skintight. It would require no pressurization since the cyborg's lungs would be partially collapsed and the blood in them cooled. Mouth and nose would be superfluous and hence sealed and non-functioning. Respiration and most other bodily processes would be effected cybernetically through the utilization of artificial organs and sensors, some of which would be attached to the exterior of the suit while others would be implanted surgically within the cyborg's body. These computerized components would serve to maintain constant pressure, temperature and metabolism within the body despite external environmental fluctuations.

The cybernaut, according to this visualization, would travel though space in a low-cost, unsealed cabin, free to move about the wastes of Mars and the moon, unmindful of radical alterations in temperature and unencumbered by heavy equipment. Chemical molecules and concentrated foods constantly spilling into the blood stream would nourish and protect him. Wastes, of course, would be recycled to make new foods, and communications would be carried on by radio propagation of electronic impulses originating in the vocal cords.

Dr. Michael Del Duca, a former NASA scientist, takes the cybernaut entirely seriously and, in fact, has enlarged on the original concept. He believes that man will eventually learn how to convert sunlight directly into energy within his own body. This sort of photosynthetic cyborg, he says, will not need any food at all and will be free to spend his entire life exploring the depths of the ocean or the far reaches of space.

Since coining the term "cyborg" in 1960, Dr. Clynes, director of the Biocybernetics Laboratory at Rockland State (which is dedicated to the computerized study of biological control functions that operate without conscious awareness in the individual), internationally acclaimed concert pianist and inventor of the widely used CAT computer, has continued to develop his concept. "The important thing to remember about the cyborg," he reflects, "is that as man changes he may no longer have at his disposal the ordinary means of expressing his humanity. So if he is to remain truly human, he must find substitute means for effecting that expression."

This means that man must first understand the essential qualities of humanness. What is the essence of a smile? of hate? of love? Can these things be defined and distilled? Dr. Clynes's startling answer is—*yes*. His studies have demonstrated that all of our perceptions and emotions have specific, measurable time-space shapes. When two or more people look at the color red they all produce the same sort of brain potentials or signals. These can be detected by delicate sensors and analyzed by a computer. Our emotions, similarly, are related to specific brain programs so that, as has been demonstrated also in Dr. Clynes's laboratory on the Hudson, computers can literally read our minds.

When we can no longer talk, smile, breathe or gesture (assuming for the purpose of this discussion that we may someday be contained not only in cybernautic capsules but perhaps even in little metal boxes), we will still be able to convey our humanity—by electronically transmitting the desired potentials to the other little metal boxes with whom we are desirous of communicating. Hence, as we lose our limbs, our noses and our other appurtenances, Dr. Clynes says, we need not lose the wealth of expressions, gestures, smiles and inflections of voice that set us apart from and presumably above the rest of the creatures of the earth. In the future, "good vibrations" will almost certainly be more than a mere expression.

And Dr. Clynes points out, an understanding of the nature of our thoughts, in terms of their mathematical, electronic and time-space (shape) identities, will permit us to communicate *better* than we do at the present time. "We may even find new shapes," he adds, "and discover means of utilizing them to communicate in entirely new ways."

Along with a growing number of computer experts, Dr. Clynes does not believe that intelligence need be confined to the DNA structure. "I believe that life is more a matter of relationships and organization than of material," he says. His conception of the intelligent, conscious computer is really a vision of the ultimate cyborg—humanity in an entirely new organizational package that may not contain a single DNA molecule. Whatever its components, it remains "human," he insists, so long as the essential inner shapes of man's psychic being and some means of transmitting them are retained.

Dr. Clynes is a man who believes that "all true progress is progress in love." Hence his lyrical and somewhat whimsical vision of the ultimate cyborg, man's humanness embodied in a computerlike package, is not surprising: "It seems likely that if computers can control their condition of awareness and optimize it with greater ease than we can in our present form, they will prefer the state of love. Since one of the characteristics of love is the desire to join with the object of love, the computers loving each other would want to merge. This will be less of a problem for computers than it is for people and will have the advantage that a combined computer could be a little better than each separately.

"There will arise, then, a succession of merging computers until there will be one enormous computer in a state of bliss, contemplating the order of nature. If this state should become difficult to maintain, in time the computer would have the choice of subdividing itself and reverting to the previous condition of multiple individuals who love each other and would tend to merge again. We actually face, then, a playful state of oscillation in which individuals unite and divide and subdivide in ever new combinations and forms. Strangely, such an image is merely an analog of nature as we see it today."

It must be made clear that the "computers" Dr. Clynes alludes to here are really cybernetic *men*. Some, however, feel that man and computer may not merge but go their separate ways, much to the detriment of the former. Is there any possibility that intelligent, *conscious* computers are likely to arise in the foreseeable future? Or are the sort of computer beings Dr. Clynes envisions *mere* whimsy? Actually, such computers are rapidly evolving in laboratories across the land and around the world right now, a new generation of machines that can read, see, talk, learn and even feel. At the University of Texas, for example, programs are being developed that will give computers sexual identities, hates, fears, loves and hopes. At Stanford, robotlike computers with hands and eyes are being constructed that can see well enough to move around obstacles, plan ahead rationally and carry out missions that have been only partially outlined by human controllers. At Mullard Research Laboratories in England, other machines are being taught to read so well that many scientists say it will be only a matter of time until they can comprehend even handwriting.

Dr. Marvin Minsky, professor of electrical engineering at MIT and a pioneer in the field of artificial intelligence, says that "our pious skeptics told us that machines would never sense things. Now that the machines can see complex shapes, our skeptics tell us that they can never know that they sense things." But he advises, "do not be bullied by authoritative pronouncements about what machines will never do. Such statements are based on pride, not fact. There has emerged no hint, in any scientific theory of machines, of limitations not shared by man. The rate of evolution of machines is millions of times faster, because we can combine separate improvements directly, where nature depends upon fortuitous events of recombination." (Genetic engineering, of course, will help man overcome part of this disadvantage, but Dr. Minsky's point is still valid: It's always going to be easier to tinker with machine than with man.)

Similarly optimistic (or pessimistic, depending on how you feel about it) is Dr. N. S. Sutherland, professor of experimental psychology at the University of Sussex and a computer expert. He states flatly that "there is a real possibility that we may one day be able to design a machine that is more intelligent than ourselves." Dr. Sutherland has made a comparative study of the basic components of the human brain and the digital-computer brain and finds the latter in several respects the more promising.

"There are all sorts of biological limitations on our own intellectual capacity," he says, "ranging from the limited number of computing elements we have available in our craniums to the limited span of human life and the slow rate at which incoming data can be accepted." Dr. Sutherland sees no such limitations in store for the computers of the future. No one is certain how many bits of permanently retrievable information the conscious portion of the human mind can accommodate in a lifetime, but many scientists think one billion is a reasonable estimate. Existing computers can transfer that amount of data—from one magnetic memory to another—in a scant twenty minutes or less. Therefore, Dr. Sutherland points out, "it will be much easier for computers to bootstrap themselves on the experience of previous computers than it is for man to benefit from the knowledge acquired by his predecessors. Moreover, if we can design a machine more intelligent than ourselves, then, *a fortiori,* that machine will be able to design one more intelligent than itself."

The problems of integration with computers equal

to or surpassing man in intelligence and sensory perception are on the minds of many scientists. "In fifty years' time," Dr. Sutherland says, "we may cease to worry about our racial problems and commense to argue over whether intelligent computers should be given the vote." Dr. J. P. Eckert, a vice-president of UNIVAC, a division of Sperry Rand Corporation, shares the same hopes—and fears. He believes that within the next half century, robot-like computers will be able to translate languages efficiently, operate typewriters, file information from voice commands, teach school, monitor patients in hospitals or at home (over telephone wires, if need be) and operate all phases of factory work.

"Memory, eyes, ears, hands and logic," he says, "have already developed to a point where they are about as good or better than man's. Recognition ability, certain types of information retrieval and the ability to taste and smell are still things in which humans excel. The electronic industries and the food industries are spending millions to solve these problems, however, and probably will in the next fifty years. At this point, man will build really general-purpose machines, universal robots. Following his experience with large calculators and teaching machines, man will know how to carry on two-way communication with them.

"I hope we have solved the integration problems between the human races," he continues, "before we face the problems of integration with robots. Our real test probably lies beyond the next fifty years, however, when mankind has developed a self-reproducing automaton that can improve itself."

Clarke is one who believes that if we do integrate successfully—to the point of actually merging with the computers to become cyborgs—we could evolve into God-like creatures.

Discussing the extraterrestrial superintelligence that is felt but unseen throughout the film *2001: A Space Odyssey* (based on his short story "The Sentinel" and co-created by himself and director Stanley Kubrick), Clarke goes even further than Dr. Clynes. Clarke conceives of that superintelligence as a presence in the universe whose evolution from man to cyborg and beyond may characterize our own future evolution, provided we avoid environmental or nuclear annihilation. First, he says, these extraterrestrials "stored" their bodies in computerlike machines, then only their brains, discarding all their natural appendages. Finally, he continues, they ceased even to be machine entities and learned to store knowledge in the "structure of space itself, and to preserve their thoughts for eternity in frozen lattices of light. They became creatures of radiation, free at last from the tyranny of matter."

Utopian as Dr. Clynes's meiotic machines and Clarke's lattices of intelligent light seem, they may not be nearly so remote as one might at first think. A quick look at cyborg development (taken into account with the computer developments just reviewed) reveals that man's probable successor has come a long way in remarkably short time. Edwin G. Johnsen, chief of the Equipment Branch of the Atomic Energy Commission/ NASA Nuclear Propulsion Office just outside Washington, D.C., and William R. Corliss, a physicist, have chronicled the genesis of dozens of man-machine systems in a survey for NASA's office of Technology Utilization.

"At first we had a hell of a time settling on a name for these things," Johnsen says, explaining that "cyborg" covers the field but has an ominous ring to it. Numerous proposals got the ax, including such labels as "manipulators," "remote-control devices" and "robots." Manipulators, Johnsen says, is too narrow a concept, since it excludes machines that are actually worn by the human operator, such as powered exoskeletons. Remote control is too broad, including as it does, everything that man does at a distance, such as changing a TV channel from his armchair. Robots are preprogramed automatons and are not linked to humans in any way. Finally the two struck on "teleoperator," which they defined as a "general-purpose, dexterous, cybernetic machine." They added that the "man-machine systems that fall through our semantical sieves allow man to: pick up and examine samples of lunar surface while remaining on earth; repair underwater oil pipelines from a surface ship; manipulate radioactive nuclear fuel elements in a hot cell; lift a ton-sized load (the man-amplifier concept); regain dexterity with an artificial limb (the prosthetics concept)" and, as we shall see, much more.

"We went from the concept of a simple master-slave manipulator in a hot cell back in the mid-40s," Johnsen explains, "to systems under development now that will project and amplify man's senses and manipulative capabilities to remote and hostile environments without endangering the man himself." This sort of total man-machine partnership, he adds, "is essential to the large-scale exploitation of space and the oceans."

Engineers at General Electric's Specialty Handling Products Operation in Schenectady, New York, agree. For the past few years they have been developing an extensive line of CAMS—Cybernetic Anthropomorphous Machine Systems, whose qualifications as cyborgs are unimpeachable. One of the first of these was "Handyman," a "master-slave" system used for handling radioactive materials that consists of two sets of arms. The human half of the system traps himself into the exoskeletal master arms that conform in shape and size to the other, remote set of slave arms. In this harness, the human operator enjoys a sense of spatial correspondence and force feedback that permits him to remotely control the "slaved" mechanical arms— through electronic links—as if they were actual extensions of his own body. Spatial correspondence causes the slaved arms to mimic every motion of the master arms. And force feedback, transmitted through sensors in the mechanical hands and detected in force reflectors in the control harness, allows the operator to "feel" objects being picked up or touched, thus enabling him to gauge and control the amount of force necessary for each task.

Once Handyman and other master-slaves had demonstrated the feasibility of hand-arm teleoperators, researchers naturally began experimenting with leg-foot systems, as well. The work was spurred on by the U. S. Army's request for a feasibility model of a CAM quadruped capable of carrying five hundred pounds through rough, off-road terrain with the agility of a mountain goat, or something approaching it. The result of the $1 million project was fueled up with gas and "loaded" with its human component—GE's Ralph S. Mosher, a mechanical engineer who has been pioneering in the cyborg field for fifteen years—and taken through its paces. At first glance the Walking Truck, as this particular CAM is called, looks like a four-legged robot, a gleaming metal monster that stands eleven feet high and weighs nearly three thousand pounds. It moves about on its hydraulic haunches with surprising fluidity and grace, suggesting a well-trained circus elephant. Mosher, tucked away in the beast's entrails, is more than a passenger; he is its brain and nervous system.

Strapped inside a control harness, electronically and hydraulically linked to the machine's appendages and equipped with sophisticated force reflectors and actuators, he has only to go through a simple crawling motion to make the quadruped move along, amplifying and extending his every movement. With the flick of a wrist, he can toss 175-pound railroad ties out of his path as if they were toothpicks; by slamming his foot down he can produce a 1500-pound wallop via the machine's corresponding hind leg. As Mosher puts it, "the man-machine relationship is so close that the experienced operator begins to feel as if those mechanical legs were his own; you imagine that you are actually crawling along the ground on all fours—but with incredible new strength."

Now GE, under the direction of Walter E. Gray,

manager of all the CAM projects, is setting out to build a two-legged pedipulator, capable of taking giant strides across the countryside. They have already demonstrated the feasibility of an eighteen-foot pedipulator (which, like the Walking Truck, has a man in it). "Actually," Gray says, "the two-legged version ought to be far easier to learn to operate, simply because it's more anthropomorphic. I see no reason why we couldn't build one capable of swinging through the trees, climbing hand over hand, getting down on all fours when necessary—one that could get around just like an ape or a monkey."

Mosher and Gray foresee the development of both mini and maxi versions of the pedipulator in the near future. "The Institute of Defense Analyses," Mosher says, "is very interested in the mini model." This one —which may be only a couple feet high or even smaller—is expected to come equipped with a small television "eye" and would be operated remotely by a man in a full-size control harness. The Institute Mosher speculates, probably has reconnaissance, surveillance and possibly sabotage missions in mind for the minipulator. "This little devil," he says, "ought to be able to take care of itself far better than an ordinary man," and if it gets caught its "better half" won't. In addition, its master will know when it gets caught and will be able to punch a destruct button, letting the slave serve double duty as a personnel mine.

As for the maxipulator, Gray believes that pedipulators with fifty-foot legs are not out of the question. When I asked what such a colossus would be used for, Richard Blackmer, manager of GE's Advanced Engineering Division, irreverently quipped that it "might come in handy in forty-nine-foot water." The fact is, Gray says, it would be quite a wader and, of course, could also step over some pretty impressive obstacles. Moreover, its giant strides might come in handy on the vast expanses of the moon, on other planets and even on the battlefield.

Among the most impressive of GE's many CAM projects is ARMS, a triple acronym dreamed up by Blackmer, the space expert who directed development of the fuel cells and related electrical controls for Project Gemini. What ARMS amounts to is a space repairman, an orbiting, remotely controlled CAM that will be permanently on call, ready to carry out repair, rescue and refurbishment missions in a community of synchronous satellites, manned space stations and transient spacecraft. The first phase of the project—the study phase—was called Application of Remote Manipulators in Space. The second phase, Blackmer says, "involves development of the first prototype hardware and is called the Anthropomorphous Remote Manipulator System." This is the current stage. The final, fully operational phase—perhaps only four or five years away—will be called Android on Remote Maneuvering Satellite.

Fanciful as the names are, the project is very real. Funding is being shared by the Air Force's Aero Propulsion Laboratory and NASA. As the scenario reads now, numerous CAM repairmen will orbit the earth, receiving and carrying out orders from ground control stations. Orbited by boosters such as the Titan 30, the ARMS systems will navigate on command, using directional thrusters, to rendezvous and dock with the satellite or craft in need of repairs. "Dead arms" will be used to grasp the "patient" while two intricately articulated arms and hands, which will correspond precisely to the arms and hands of a human operator on earth, will be used for the actual repair work. Television eyes located on the CAM head, which will project up out of its boxlike body, will provide the human part of the system with a stereoscopic view of the operation. In addition to this visual feedback, the earth operator will also experience force feedback so that he can feel the various components that he will be removing or repairing across 22,000 miles.

Apart from replacing batteries, exchanging tape components and experimental packages, repairing small parts that can knock out an entire satellite and so on, ARMS is expected to update a number of satellites, thus reducing the costs of early obsolescence. If there are at least 130 satellites in synchronous (permanent) orbit by 1980, as expected, savings from these operations could be considerable. GE and NASA studies indicate that seven repair jobs will more than pay for each ARMS system (which, incidentally, will be largely self-servicing). If used for astronaut rescue missions, for exploration, for in-space construction jobs or for destruction or disarming of hostile satellites, their value will be enchanced immeasurably.

Blackmer, who says he hopes to see test models flown in the early 1970s, observes that "there are no hardware obstacles in our way. We have the means at hand right now to build these things." With that in mind, it shouldn't be too difficult to imagine far more advanced space cyborgs for the near future. William E. Bradley, an engineering authority on electronics and solid-state physics and an assistant vice-president for the Institutes of Defense Analyses "think tank" in Arlington, Virginia, has coined the word "telefactoring," which he defines quite simply as "doing something at a distance." The telefactors Bradley has in mind, however, would not only perform repairs in space but explore it as well, replacing man physically though not mentally in this hazardous undertaking.

Johnsen of the Space Nuclear Propulsion Office has begun drumming up support for Bradley's concept, constantly enlarging on its possibilities. They envision telefactors that would be "slaved" in every conceivable way. Astronauts, or in this case terrenauts, strapped into control harnesses on earth could, in the Bradley-Johnsen visualization, roam through space, walk the surface of the moon, the asteroids or even Mars without "lifting off" as much as an inch. Linked by radio and television and by audio-visual, tactile, force and perhaps even olfactory and gustatory feedback to their mechanical slave doubles, they would miss nothing of the actual space experience and at the same time would risk nothing, either. And thanks to the superstrength of their mechanical proxies, they would maneuver through space and across the distant planets without weighty and expensive life-support systems.

Most of the technology necessary for telefactoring is at hand. Tactile feedback systems are still in their infancy, but promising work is underway at Stanford University's Research Institute. Scientists there recently developed finger-tip size, air-jet stimulators that may be the forerunners of sophisticated tactile systems that will extend our ability to distinguish even between the textures of silk and velvet over hundreds of thousands and perhaps even millions of miles. Force feedback already lets man determine the presence and shape of objects and to some extent their relative hardness over great distances. Head-controlled television systems providing sophisticated visual feedback have been developed by Philco and other companies and are constructed in such a way that the slave's "eyes" always look in exactly the same direction as the master's.

This leaves only the time-lag problem, in cases where master and slave are separated by millions of miles. For example, signals traveling at the speed of light (186,000 miles per second) will still take nearly three minutes to get back to earth from a telefactor on Mars, making for some serious coordination problems. In some instances, of course, this problem can be overcome simply by putting the master in an orbiting spacecraft or space station. In others, where operation from earth is necessary or desirable, Johnsen believes that move-and-wait tactics and "predictor controls" will come to the rescue. On the basis of known environmental factors, predictor devices can construct computer models that will look ahead in time and actuate appropriate feedback. Stanford, General Motors and others are already at work on such controls.

Confident that the time-lag problem will be overcome, Johnsen creates this word picture to dramatize the art of telefactoring: "Imagine a man wearing a lightweight exoskeleton to control the arms, legs and torso of a distant teleoperator and a head-controlled system (looking something like a motorcycle helmet) to control the teleoperator's television camera. The man receives back through the exoskeleton visual, audio, motion and force feedback. Microminiaturized air-jet transducers under his finger tips pick up and convey the tactile information. Now, by providing any number of duplicate exoskeletons, scientist, engineers, doctors and even the average person can vicariously participate in scientific experiments and remote exploration. Imagine, for example, 'feely TV' with thousands of remote console receivers with people wired into them, all getting the feel of digging on the moon or Mars and seeing the actual scene—while only one operator, the astronaut, is actually in the control loop, either here on earth or in orbit."

Johnsen and others believe that teleoperators of this sort will be used for terrestrial operations, as well —in disaster areas, in mining, in nuclear facilities, in warehouses, perhaps even in medicine. Doctors at Boston General Hospital, Johnsen points out, are taking very seriously the notion of telediagnosis. So far this amounts only to examining patients over closed-circuit television systems that link the hospital with the Boston airport. "But there's no reason why manipulators couldn't be attached to the television," Johnsen says, "so that the doctor could actually thump the patient on the chest, look into his ear, take his pulse and so on, all without leaving his office or wasting precious time on the road. With the advent of precision feedback, telesurgery is likely to become a reality, permitting surgeons from all over the world to plug into the system and form a team without leaving their respective countries."

Applications for this breed of cyborg are as far-ranging as the human imagination. Ultimately, it has been suggested, machines may be made to respond to the spoken word (computers exist now that do just this, though as yet on a limited scale), the slightest gesture, even to thoughts which, after all, have very precise electrical potentials that can be tapped and channeled, thus making ever more cozy the symbiosis that is quickly developing between man and machine. Already there are experimental automobile braking systems that can be activated by merely lifting an eyebrow, cutting the reaction time required by a foot-brake system by more than 50 per cent. How much longer will it be until equally quick and unobtrusive physiological mechanisms control acceleration, steering and so on, until, as Clarke puts it, man *becomes* the machine?

Amputees now have at their disposal artificial limbs that are actuated by thought. Developed by researchers at Harvard and MIT, motors in the artificial arm pick up electrical signals from the brain so that when the amputee wishes to raise his arm he has only to think about it and up it goes. The military is now experimenting with mounted guns (some in use on helicopters) that are linked to the human eye, following its movements with precision. At the press of a button or very firm flick of the eye, the gun fires at and invariably hits whatever the human eye is focusing on. So much for that old line: "*If* looks could kill. . . ." Less frightening, but even more intriguing, is work underway at the Burden Neurological Institute in Bristol, England, where researchers have linked human brains with computers, via the use of harmless electrodes, and have demonstrated that brain waves can start and stop machines and even "instruct" them to perform specific tasks.

Finally, some scientists are convinced, human brains will be implanted in computerized mechanical bodies, achieving what has been called "total prosthesis." The proposition that a brain can be sustained in the living state outside the body is supported by the experiments of Dr. Robert J. White of Western Reserve University in Cleveland, among others. Dr. White succeeded in maintaining a number of monkey brains in isolation. As for actually putting a human brain into a computerized body, such noted scientists as Dr. James Bonner, a Caltech biologist active in genetics, scarcely blink at the suggestion. When brains become too large (through genetic engineering) to carry around comfortably, Dr. Bonner says, what is to prevent us from coming up with brains "that will stay in one place and send their sense organs out into the world?" In fact, he adds there might be spectacular advantages to computerized bodies (beyond the obvious) such as acquisition of entirely new sense organs. Acquisition of an organ for sending and receiving microwave signals, for example, "would be very convenient for communications at a distance," he says. So Clarke is not the only one who thinks that man may one day become, in effect, something as improbable as a radio or television station.

Man's marriage to machine, however, is expected to do more than extend his senses, amplify his strength and optimize his efficiency. Though all of these things will assist man in the exploration of outer space, it is equally important that he explore the inner space of his own mind, of hate, love, pleasure, pain, grief and all the other planets of the psyche. The cyborg must be an extraordinary calculating machine but, more important, he must also be an extraordinary *thinking* machine, enjoying easy access to and command over the vast spectrum of human thoughts and emotions.

This command is already being partially achieved in experiments underway in California. Dr. Joe Kamiya, a San Francisco psychologist associated with Langley Porter Neuropsychiatric Institute, has "taught" people to "feel" and sustain at will a certain state of mind that is achieved by accomplished Zen Buddhists during deep meditation. This is the so-called "alpha state" (characterized by the alpha brain-wave rhythm of eight to thirteen cycles per second), a state of wakeful suspension that reportedly suffuses the subject with profound serenity, deep relaxation and a drifting, floating sensation of pleasure.

The teaching procedure was simple but ingenious. Dr. Kamiya wired his volunteers to EEG machines that would write out their brain waves and activate buzzers whenever they slipped into the alpha state. Slowly the subjects began to recognize the interior geography of the alpha state and then rapidly learned to turn it on and off at will. Some became so adept at this that they could make the buzzer ring almost instantly at Dr. Kamiya's command, indicating awesome command over the subtle variation of the thoughts and emotions that induce alpha rhythm.

Researchers at the Sepulveda Veterans Administration Hospital in southern California have come up with a refinement on the Kamiya technique, using colored lights instead of buzzers as the cerebral feedback. When a volunteer is on an "alpha high" (the technology is breeding a whole new set of cultlike jargon to rival that of the drug culture) the EEG machine activates a blue light that projects onto a motion-picture screen. The scientists there are rapidly coding other colors with other states of mind so that the human subject can learn to recognize and control the whole spectrum of emotions. Dr. Julius Segal, a psychologist with the National Institutes of Mental Health, predicts that "portable EEG trainers" will become available in the near future. In fact, he says, they may very well become standard equipment in bedrooms across the land, enabling the average individual to "hook up" and—by watching his thoughts play across a screen—psyche himself out and gradually take command over his emotions.

The EEG trainer suggests something even more utopian. For if the cybernetic organism can transmit and project electronic potentials he should also be able to receive them. Researchers specializing in the field of electronic stimulation of the brain (ESB) have demonstrated that this is, in fact, the case. It is possible to implant stainless steel electrodes into the brains of humans and by pulsing electric current through them from remote transmitters control various aspects of their behavior. Rats whose pleasure centers were wired in this way were, in a number of experiments, permitted to activate the stimulating current themselves simply by pressing a lever with their forepaws. And press it they did—thousands of times a day for weeks on end, experiencing pleasures that obviously eclipsed those of mere sex, food and drink, for the rats gave up on the first completely and took only the briefest breaks for the second and third. Humans, wired for various medical reasons, have reported similarly pleasurable experiences. Others have undergone "experiential hallucinations," reliving former episodes of their lives so vividly that, for all practical purposes, they had done the "impossible" and gone back into the past. Stimulation of some parts of the brain evoked similar hallucinations—but ones that obviously could not have had any basis in fact.

Because electrodes can be implanted with such precision (even into a single brain cell), many scientists believe that thousands of synthetic experiences could be made available to an individual with a sufficent number of electrodes implanted in his brain. Hence, in a few decades, it is not unthinkable that man—the cyborg—will have a few hundred electrodes implanted into his brain shortly after birth and that each home will be equipped with an "experience synthesizer," "dream machine" or whatever industry chooses to call this successor to television and the movies. The "wired" individual will have only to sit down at the synthesizer console, consult a directory of experiences (perhaps categorized G, M, R, X), make his selection (an evening with the current sex symbol, a climb up Mount Everest, total oblivion or whatever strikes his fancy), dial the appropriate code number for the selection into a remote, centralized computer shared by the whole community and sit back and enjoy, climb, float or whatever. All in all, a pleasant interlude on our way to becoming lattices of light, *if* we make it.

# AFTERWORD

Brave New Baby and
the Population
Explosion

In the course of this book, I have taken note of a number of great advances in biological sciences, advances that promise to catapult man from creature to creator—*provided* he avoids the many perils that accompany the promise. And a number of those dangers have been inventoried, too. But the greatest danger man faces at this point in his development is overpopulation—and the attendant horrors of a deteriorating environment. The Biological Revolution that has been the subject of this book can contribute to the disaster that seems increasingly imminent—or it can help circumvent it. One thing is certain: The advances discussed here will never be exploited—except, perhaps, by a privileged few—unless something is done first to check population growth and environmental decay. Without these things, a number of eminent scientists warn, there will be no future at all.

First, let's examine the scope of the problem. It is generally estimated that the population of the earth was somewhere around 2.5 million in the year 1,000,000 B.C. By 6000 B.C. this figure had doubled to 5 million people. By A.D. 1650 there were about 500 million people, which means that the population after 6000 B.C. had doubled approximately every 1000 years. Then it reached a billion in 1850, the doubling time having diminished to only 200 years. That is alarming enough, but over the next eighty years the population doubled in size once again, reaching 2 billion around 1930. Now world population is well over 3 billion and the doubling time is a scant 37 years or less. Many population experts say we will have 7 billion people by the turn of the century—if we survive that long, if the environment can stand up under the strain.

If we were to keep on reproducing at the present rate, Dr. Paul Ehrlich, the noted Stanford University population biologist, declares that we would have 60 million billion people in another 900 years —"or about 100 persons for each square foot of the earth's surface." Obviously this can never happen. Something will have to give—and that something is not likely to be very pleasant. If man will not step in to check his own proliferation, famine, plague or nuclear war will.

Well, what about moving to some other planet— before we breed to death on this one? Forget it. Professor Garrett Hardin of the University of California at Santa Barbara has marshaled the facts and figures that would be involved in such an exodus and has come up with the discouraging news that even if Americans were willing to reduce their standard of living to 18 per cent of its present level, they could still only export to the nearest stars *one day's* increase in the population *each year*.

And even if we did somehow manage to get to the other planets, Dr. Ehrlich says, "in a few thousand years, at the current growth rate, all the material in the visible universe would have been converted into people, and the sphere of people would be expanding outward at the speed of light!"

Another, perhaps more dangerous, panacea is the notion that the so-called "Green Revolution" will feed the masses even without population control. The Green Revolution is based on the development and massive exploitation of new high-yield grains. Unfortunately, this is a revolution that is likely to fall flat, crushing millions under its weight. The development of these new "miracle" grains has already had the ominous effect of lulling many into believing that we don't have to worry about the population explosion, that science is coming to the rescue, that there will *always* be enough for everyone to eat.

Yet, at best, the Green Revolution can only be a stopgap measure, buying perhaps fifteen or twenty years for the starving millions. And if Green Revolutions (without attendant population control) of the past are any indication of what is to come, then the purchase of that time will prove a poor investment, indeed. One need only look at the Green Revolution created by the potato in Ireland two centuries ago to understand this. Like the Green Revolutions of today, the Irish variety depended on massive plantings of a single type of food, creating what biologists call "mono-cultures." Without genetic variability in crops, it becomes increasingly difficult to stay ahead of the bugs and pests. The more simplified the "culture," the more vulnerable it—and those who depend upon it—are to natural pests and predators. (Already becoming legend is the new breed of "miracle rats" that has arisen in the wake of the "miracle rice" recently introduced in the Philippines.)

In Ireland it was another sort of "miracle"—the potato—that led to disaster. After it was introduced, at the expense of other crops, the impoverished two million people living there rapidly bred up to about eight million. Then along came the potato blight. With nothing to fall back on, two million people died of starvation and another two million fled—emigrating to distant lands. Today, of course, there is no place left to emigrate to—so the ironical consequence of providing a new food to two million people *without* population control, under the same circumstances, would be the ultimate deaths of four million people! Even *with* population control, the Green Revolution, based on mono-cultures, is ecologically unsound in the all-important long run; *without* population control it is sheer lunacy.

"Family planning" is another dangerous concept, dangerous because it, too, gives us a false sense of security. The prevention of all *unwanted* children, the goal of the family planning concept, would be admirable if it were not for the fact that most people confuse this with adequate population control. The fact is, people *want* too many children. Hence, even if family planning were to be 100 per cent successful, and it is a long way from that today, there would still exist a very severe population problem.

Too many people. Too many "solutions" that actually aggravate the problem. What does all of this mean in practical terms? It means that since 1958 population has been increasing faster than the food supply, that already ten to twenty million people are starving to death, that an estimated three-fourths of the world goes to bed hungry each night. It's little wonder that many scientists are coming to believe that the medical and biological sciences have their priorities all wrong, that much of what passes for "humanitarian" research is really quite the opposite. Untold millions, for example, are being spent in the effort to overcome heart disease and cancer, to prolong the lives of the crippled, the deformed and the aged, while almost nothing is being done about overpopulation. It is here that some of the scientists working to create the world of Brave New Baby find themselves in a moral bind.

"There may well come a time when even as humane a society as ours will find that people with inherited diseases constitute a social burden so great to our relative resources that we will be forced to limit what most of us consider one of our inalienable rights—the right to bear children without reference to the consequences of society. We already do this to a limited extent when we isolate certain categories of feeble-minded, insane and criminal individuals—and thus prohibit their reproduction." These are the words of George and Muriel Beadle (the former a Nobel Prize winner) in *The Language of Life*.

Dr. Theodosius Dobzhansky voices similar concern in *Heredity and the Nature of Man*. "It is a depressing thought," he says, "that we are helping the ailing, the lame, the deformed, only to make our descendants more ailing, more lame and more deformed." Those who introduced the potato into Ireland two hundred years ago could not have foreseen the disastrous consequences of that seemingly simple, judicious and humanitarian action. Today's scientists cannot fall back on ignorance as an excuse for what they do; the more thoughtful of them know that medical aid to underdeveloped countries, for example, will almost certainly, in the absence of population control (resisted in many of these countries on religious grounds), result in far greater death and suffering later on. By prolonging life and building up the population *now* they contribute to the magnitude of the disaster that will occur when food runs out *later;* in fact, they hurry the day of that disaster.

By the same token, such things as heart transplants, artificial organs and other innovations of the Biological Revolution designed to prolong life begin to look a little ridiculous, perhaps even sinister, in light of the population crisis. This does not mean that we should give up forever the ideal of a world free of disease; but it does mean that we must *first* strive for a world with a *manageable, stable* population.

Fortunately, the medical and biological advances of the past few decades need not always aggravate the population problem; they also possess the potential of helping overcome it. It was earlier suggested, for example, that genetic engineering might make it possible one day for the breeding of a new sort of man, one capable of coping with pollutants that presently impair health, one able to tap the energy of the sun directly, one compact in size and thus "economical" in terms of his demands on the environment, and so on. These things are by no means out of the question, provided they are desired by enough people and provided that we have the considerable time that would be necessary to achieve them.

Time, however, is short, and it is certain that radical changes in the human genotype—designed to accommodate a deteriorating environment—will not be possible for several decades. Even with them, it is apparent that population must be checked sooner or later. Without them, population must be checked *now*. The means, if not the resolve, to do this are at hand —or very nearly at hand. The Pill and other birth-control devices have at least partially destroyed the traditional notion that sex and reproduction must go hand in hand. Refinement of the "morning-after" pill, the male birth-control pill and long-term birth-control injections will further attenuate this idea and thus, hopefully, contribute to a smaller population. Research in this field must be given top priority, as should research aimed at the development of psychopharmacological agents that provide substitutes for the sexual satisfaction many women derive from childbearing.

It is well established that many women experience a nearly overwhelming urge to bear a child. As was seen in the first chapter of this book, it is a need felt most keenly by women who have been unable to have *any* children. A woman somehow denied the opportunity to fulfill her biological role and become a mother in many instances feels that she is not fully a woman. But some of the startling advances being made in the field of electronic and chemical stimulation of the brain, discussed in the last section of this book, make it seem probable that even such powerful, inbred needs as this could be overcome with an appropriate pill. Doesn't it seem more practical, at any rate, to spend millions in search of such a chemical than to spend the same money trying to perfect a heart-transplant operation to prolong the lives of a few mostly elderly —and mostly wealthy—individuals?

Sex selection—discussed in Chapter Three of Part One—is another area in which the Biological Revolution can contribute to the fight against runaway population. Fortunately, as we have seen, a procedure has already been developed by which parents can, with high expectation of success, choose the sex of their offspring. While such procedures are not the answer to the whole problem, population biologists are confident that many parents will use them to limit their families to one boy and one girl.

Throughout this book I have suggested the need for a number of new federal agencies to regulate such things as cloning, embryo implantations, the screening of genetic defects, sperm banks, sex ratios, genetic manipulation and so on. Far more pressing is the need for an agency with the power to control the size of the population, having first determined what the ideal size is, at any given time. One of its most important functions would be to promote research directed at development of better birth-control agents, possibly even of mass sterilants.

Most scientists hope that compulsory birth control will never become necessary. But if it ever should— and it is looking more and more like it will—one frequently proposed method involves the addition of a sterilant to public drinking water, much as we add chloride and, in some areas, fluoride today. Couples wishing to conceive would be required to apply for a license from the government. If they met all the necessary qualifications and if there existed a need for an additional birth in a particular area at that time, the government agency involved would issue the couple an *antidote* to the substance in the water. This would enable them to successfully conceive a child, even though they would continue to drink public water. The antidote, of course, would rapidly wear off, so that they could not go on having children without again applying for a license to do so.

Such an agency would also be designed to encourage further research in sex selection, work to obtain and enforce federal legislation guaranteeing every one desiring it the right to voluntary sterilization and the right to abortion regardless of the circumstances, seek mandatory sex education in the schools and provide tax incentives to those who refrain from having children (thus reversing our present system of tax exemptions for children). Until some agency exists to coordinate the effort to control population—and one with the power to contain the population—there is really no hope of progress or, at any rate, of *lasting* progress. If such procedures seem coercive, consider the alternative. And having done that, it might be wise to accept the rationale underlying Nobelist F. H. C. Crick's contention that "having children ought to be at least as much a matter of public concern as driving a car," which long ago required a license.

Finally perhaps, despite the many difficulties that lie ahead, we can justifiably comfort ourselves, after a fashion, with the knowledge that we are living in what may well be the most important era in the history of life on this planet. Dr. W. H. Thorpe, the prominent Cambridge University ethologist, has summed up the world we are living in—and the one we are just entering—in these words:

"The ethical problems raised by the population explosion and artificial imsemination, by genetics and neurophysiology, and by the social and mental sciences are at least as great as those arising from atomic energy and the H-bomb, from space travel and ultrasonic flight, from telecommunications, computers and automation. There is no doubt in my mind that several of these developments are as epoch-making for mankind as any that have preceded them. They rank at least as high, if not higher, in importance than the discovery of fire, of agriculture, the development of printing and the discovery of the wheel."

# Glossary

*Age pigments*—Stray bits of cellular molecules believed by some scientists to effect cell death by attaching themselves to the long-chain molecules vital to normal cell functioning.

*Amniocentesis*—The withdrawal and testing of a sample of the *amniotic fluid* that surrounds the fetus in the womb; an office procedure involving puncture of the abdominal wall with a special needle. The fluid provides valuable clues about the health of the fetus.

*Anabolics*—Synthetic hormones that have a physically rejuvenating effect, particularly on the elderly.

*Androsperm*—Sperm that carry the Y sex chromosome and thus produce male offspring.

*Apgar scale*—A battery of tests used to determine the health of newborns; named after its developer, Dr. Virginia Apgar.

*Artificial chimera*—A term used to describe an organism, derived through genetic manipulation, of mixed genetic material; in Greek mythology, a she-monster with a lion's head, a goat's body and a serpent's tail.

*Artificial inovulation*—Artificial insertion of egg into the uterus or fallopian tubes; applications are indicated in cases where women do not produce viable egg cells of their own and thus cannot achieve pregnancy under normal circumstances.

*Artificial insemination*—Artificial insertion of sperm into the vagina or cervix; used in instances of infertility that result from the husband's inability to produce viable sperm cells. Sperm is furnished by an anonymous donor who, typically, is paid for his services by the doctor performing the insemination.

*Artificial intelligence*—A theory that posits that intelligent cognition need not be the exclusive property of living matter, that it can be artificially engendered within the organization of advanced computers and other mechanical devices. Intelligent computers predicted by many scientists would have the ability to reproduce themselves.

*Artificial placenta*—Any of a number of mechanical devices currently under development that are designed to monitor and control the exchange of nutrients and waste between mother and fetus.

*Artificial womb*—A device that would incorporate an artificial placenta and maintain the fetus, outside its natural womb, through gestation to birth; popularly envisioned in Aldous Huxley's science-fiction novel *Brave New World* and now under development at a number of centers.

*Asexual propagation*—Reproduction without the intermingling of male and female sex cells. See *cloning*.

*Auto-adultery*—A term coined to describe techniques by which females can conceivably fertilize their own eggs or cause them to start dividing to produce a new individual without benefit of male sperm.

*Bench embryos*—Refers to embryos "jettisoned" or discarded at the bench (in the laboratory) after *sexing techniques,* in which all but the embryo of the desired sex are destroyed. Multiple embryos, to choose from, are obtained through superovulation and artificial insemination.

*Biocybernetics*—The computerized study of biological control functions that operate without conscious awareness in the individual.

*Body cells*—Cells which, unlike sex cells, contain the full complement of forty-six chromosomes; also called *soma cells*.

*Brain waves*—Electrical activity within the brain that is categorized by electroencephalogram in terms of frequency and amplitude. Distinct brain-wave rhythms include *delta, theta, alpha* and *beta,* in order of ascending frequencies. Brain-wave activity in the human falls within a spectrum of zero to forty cycles per second in frequency.

*Capacitation*—A phenomenon, apparently chemical in nature, by which the sperm is rendered capable of fertilizing the egg. Whether the capacitating agent is wholly or partly contained within the sperm or whether it is contained within the vaginal or cervical secretions is not yet fully understood in the human. Illumination of this technique promises new and possibly much better approaches to birth control.

*Cell-death theory*—The idea that aging is the consequence of random failure and death of cells throughout the body; when enough cells die, according to this theory, the entire organism dies.

*Centrifugation*—A technique employing centrifugal force to separate substances of differing densities; used, in animal experiments, to separate male- and female-producing sperm cells. Cells thus separated are then used to artificially inseminate cattle with the desired sex.

*Chromosome*—Unit of heredity contained within the cell nucleus; each body cell contains forty-six chromosomes, half of which come from the male and half from the female. Chromosomes contain the smaller *genes* and *nucleotides* which determine physical and mental characteristics, such as sex, skin color, mental capacity and so on.

*Clomid*—A fertility drug that stimulates ovarian follicles in such a way that they release eggs that otherwise would be retained; used to achieve pregnancies in cases that previously resisted all treatment. But like another drug in this class called *Perganol,* which contains *follicle-stimulating hormone* (FSH), it often results in multiple pregnancies.

*Cloning*—A method of asexual propagation by which body cells, rather than sex cells, divide to create a new individual. Fertilization or pollination plays no role in clonal reproduction. Clonal offspring have only one parent and are genetically identical to that parent. Cloning has been achieved in certain vegetables and lower animal forms; scientists predict its use with mammals including man.

*Cross-species memory transplants*—The transplantation from one species to another of molecules suspected to be the chemical residing place of memory; pioneering experiments suggest the feasibility of such "transplants," suggesting that man, in the remote future, may be able to experience the "thoughts" of lower animal forms.

*Cryogenics*—Study of production and effects of very low temperatures; some hope that cryogenic freezing can be used to achieve *animated suspension,* in which life functions are slowed or halted but life itself is preserved.

*Culdoscopy*—A diagnostic technique employing the culdoscope, an instrument through which one can view internal bodily organs without surgical incision. The culdoscope is passed through the posterior fornix of the vagina into the peritoneal cavity. The pencil-sized scope carries its own light, channeled through thousands of nearly microscopic fibers *(fibers optics,)* and can be used to examine ovaries and fallopian tubes in cases where disease is suspected. *Operative culdoscopy* employs, along with the scope, tiny surgical tools that can be manipulated from outside the body, again obviating surgical incisions.

*Cybernaut*—A cybernetic organism specifically designed for space travel, reducing the amount of encumbering life-support systems used by the conventional astronaut; also called *space cyborg.*

*Cybernetic anthropomorphous machines*—CAMS, as they are called, are *man-machine symbiotes* designed for specific tasks; man, in these systems, serves as the central nervous system while the machine amplifies his every movement through anthropomorphic mechanical extensions. A class of cyborg.

*Cybernetics*—Comparative study of the automatic control system formed by the nervous system and brain and by mechanical-electrical communications systems.

*Cyborg*—A cybernetic organism; any of a number of systems in which man and machine are intimately linked so that the machine becomes a natural extension of the man requiring little or no conscious effort to control.

*Dance of love*—A term popularized by Dr. Landrum B. Shettles to describe micrographs depicting sperm trying to enter the egg. Thousands of sperm penetrate the outer core of the egg and lash their tails in rhythmic waves trying to get to its nucleus. But only one penetrates to the center of the egg, owing to some as yet unexplained mechanism within the egg itself. It is this mechanism, however, that permits *fertilization* by only one sperm to take place.

*Decompression*—A technique by which, according to some medical claims, intelligence of the newborn can be enhanced. Women are placed in small decompression chambers during various phases of pregnancy, a procedure that presumably increases the amount of oxygen that is fed through the placenta to the fetus in the womb.

*DNA*—Deoxyribonucleic acid is the repository of hereditary information. Its long, double-stranded molecules, twisted in the shape of a spiral staircase, are composed of the nucleotides, chemicals that go into making up the genes.

*Ecdysone*—Also known as the *Peter Pan hormone,* this is the substance that controls the metamorphosis of many insects from larval to adult form. It can be used to artificially retard metamorphosis and escalate adolescent growth.

*Ecology*—A branch of science concerned with the interrelationships of organisms and their environment.

*Ectogenesis*—The entire process of "test-tube pregnancy" from *in-vitro* fertilization of the egg to expulsion of the fetus from an artificial womb.

*Education by injection*—A concept promulgated by the experiments of James V. McConnell and others, in which planarians, trained to wend their way through a maze, were chopped up and fed to untrained planarians who then negotiated the maze without any difficulty. The injection of brain RNA molecules from one organism to another.

*Electrochemical theory of memory*—A theory that says memory is first encoded in neuro-electrical circuits within the brain and then, for permanent storage, encoded in chemical molecules within the brain cells. The search for the so-called *"memory molecule"* continues, with major interest centering on RNA.

*Electroencephalogram*—The tracing, on graph paper, of brain waves picked up, via electrodes, by an electro-encephalograph (EEG) machine. The electrodes are attached to the scalp with a special conductive glue.

*Electronic stimulation of the brain*—Direct electrical stimulation of the brain via implanted electrodes; used to treat various disorders such as rage, epileptic seizures, pain. May also be used to create in the mind of the subject a wide range of experiences.

*Electrophoresis* — Movement of suspended particles through a fluid effected by electronic force; used in a partially successful attempt to separate male- and female-producing types of sperm.

*Embryo*—The developing human individual from the time of implantation in the uterus to the end of the first eight weeks of gestation. Thereafter, the individual is called a *fetus*.

*Embryo implant*—Implantation of an embryo into the uterus by artificial means; promises to help women with a variety of health problems have children of their own, where such would not have been possible or practical in the past. Implants from one woman to another are contemplated.

*Endometriosis*—A disease of women in which the ovaries and fallopian tubes become inoperative due to agglutination caused by accumulation of stray but growing pieces of *endometrium,* material that generally is found only in the lining of the uterus. Its cause is not yet known.

*Enzyme*—Complex substances produced by living cells that bring about or accelerate numerous reactions at the molecular level. Their absence can result in troublesome and often fatal *enzyme-deficiency diseases*.

*Enzyme xerography*—A term that has been used to apply to the possible manufacture of enzymes through viral reproduction.

*Erythroblastosis fetalis*—Also known as *Rh disease*. The Rh factor is present in about 85 per cent of the population. When it is present, the blood is said to be Rh positive; when absent, Rh negative. When an Rh-negative woman bears an Rh-positive baby (as a result of mating with an Rh-positive male), her body may become sensitized and develop *antibodies* to fend off the "foreign" invaders. These antibodies attack the fetus' erythrocytes or red-blood cells.

*Estrogen*—Female sex hormone, important in the development of secondary sexual characteristics and in the maintenance of the female reporductive cycle.

*Eugenics*—A science concerned with the improvement of hereditary qualities. *Negative eugenics* seeks to eliminate hereditary defects that have already manifested themselves in the breed. *Positive eugenics* actively seeks to improve the stock through controlled breeding.

*Experiential hallucinations*—Hallucinations that recapitulate actual experiences so that the individual feels that he is actually reliving that experience. Experiential hallucinations have been induced with electrical stimulation of the brain through implanted electrodes.

*Family planning*—A concept revolving around the prevention of all unwanted children through the use of contraceptives and contraceptive information; sometimes referred to as *planned parenthood*. Family planning is not synonymous with *population control*, which requires a balancing of death and birth rates.

*Feedback*—Technically, the return to the input of a part of the output of a machine, system or process. Feedback is what permits an individual to gauge the amount of force needed to lift an object, open a door, etc. The resistance the individual encounters is fed back to his brain which, in turn, makes adjustments in the muscles via the central nervous system. There are many types of feedback: visual, audio, force, tactile, olfactory, etc. Feedback is of extreme importance in man-machine symbiosis.

*Fetology*—A relatively new medical subspecialty, the primary concern of which is the fetus and its development. *Fetologists* use amniocentesis and other techniques to monitor the progress of the fetus. Treatment for fetal ills ranges from injection of drugs into the amniotic sac (where they are gradually ingested) to actual removal and surgical manipulation of the fetus.

*Fimbriae*—The fingerlike projections of the fallopian tubes that hover over the ovaries and "pick up" the egg when it is ejected from its follicle each month.

*Genetic counseling*—An organized effort to identify genetic defects that could be passed on to prospective offspring; particularly valuable for couples who have already produced a defective child or who, by virtue of age or family history, are more likely than others to produce a defective. Chromosomes are examined microscopically, and counselors advise prospective parents about their chances of giving birth to a deformed or otherwise defective child.

*Genetic engineering*—The mechanical or biochemical manipulation of the basic units of heredity, the chromosomes, genes and nucleotides, to effect specific changes or new developments in the incipient individual. *Genetic surgery,* which falls into this category, may be used to correct hereditary defects or to provide desired physical and mental characteristics in the individual. Gene insertion, deletion and modification will all figure in genetic surgery.

*Genotype*—A class or group of individuals sharing a specified genetic makeup; the basic model of man.

*Germinal choice*—A program of positive eugenics proposed by the late Dr. H. J. Muller, Nobel Prize man, in which women desiring children would be required to undergo artificial insemination with the sperm of genetically superior men; these women would be provided with detailed dossiers on the approved donors and afforded some choice in the selection of the donor in each case.

*Green Revolution*—A term applied to the development and use of new hybrid grains noted for their high yields. Proponents of the "revolution" claim that it will rescue from famine the ever-growing masses. Critics deny this, pointing out that the "Green Revolution" depends on the establishment of vast mono-cultures, dense plantings of single crops with a minimum of genetic variability and, thus, a maximum vulnerability to pests and plant diseases.

*Gynosperm*—Sperm cells that carry the X sex chromosome and thus produce female offspring.

*Hermaphroditism*—Condition in plant or animal of having both male and female reproductive organs.

*Hibernation*—A torpid resting state; a type of suspended animation in which vital life functions are markedly slowed; proposed by some as a superior alternative to

cryogenic suspension in the effort to prolong life or reduce demands on life-support systems during long space
journeys.

*Homosexual unions*—A term coined by the late Dr. Jean
Rostand to describe some of the bizarre results of sexual manipulation. "Using salamanders and toads," Dr.
Rostand said, "false females [genetic males transformed into females with sex hormones [have been
coupled with true males and false males with true
females, and from these unions descendants have been
obtained that were the issue of two fathers or two
mothers."

*Hormone*—A product of living cells that circulates
throughout the cells and produces activity at points
remote from its place of origin; important in growth,
maturation, sexual differentiation.

*Hybrid*—Offspring of two animals or plants of differing
species; *hybridization* is the process of intermingling
different species to produce new types of individuals.

*Hydrocephalus*—An abnormality in which excessive fluid
accumulates within the cranial cavity; a concern of
fetologists, who are devising new methods of treatment.

*Immune system*—A system of the body in which *gamma
globulin,* a fraction of blood plasma, produces antibodies which attack and destroy foreign bodies, toxins,
bacteria and the like; some studies indicate that the
immune system can be altered during fetal development in such a way that the body will later tolerate
tissue and organ transplants without sparking the rejection syndrome.

*Infertility*—Inability to produce offspring. Clinically, a
couple is said to be infertile after trying to have a
child, without success, for two years. *Sterility* is a term
that is clinically applied only in those cases where
absolute infertility is indicated by complete failure to
produce sperm or egg cells, lack of reproductive organs,
etc.

*In-vitro fertilization*—Literally, fertilization "in glass,"
meaning test-tube fertilization; in-vitro fertilization, the
first step in ectogenesis, has been achieved with a
variety of animals, including man.

*Ion*—An atom or group of atoms that carries a positive
or negative electrical charge as a result of having

gained or lost one or more of its electrons. Some experiments indicate that negatively ionized air can enhance physical vigor and mental acuity and possibly even prolong life.

*Karyotyping*—Qualitative and quantitative examination of cell nucleus components, specifically the chromosomes; the chromosomes, derived from cells grown in culture mediums, are examined microscopically, photographed and magnified to reveal possible chromosome breaks, linkages, etc., used in genetic counseling.

*Male birth-control pill*—Most attempts at developing male contraceptive pills have had only limited success. The chemicals, most of which inhibit the production of spermatozoa, have undesirable side effects, such as loss of sexual desire. Though many scientists predict a workable male birth-control pill for the future, others believe men will resist using them for psychological reasons.

*Man-amplifiers*—Mechanized extensions of man that amplify his strength; man is linked to the system with a series of feedback mechanisms. See *cyborg.*

*Memory banks*—A futuristic concept involving the storage of memory molecules. *"Mind libraries,"* it has been suggested, might house such molecules, rather than books, marking them available to the public or specific segments of the public. With refinement, ingestion or injection of such molecules would presumably permit an individual to "tune in" on the mind and memories of another individual.

*Memory erasure*—Literally, chemical brainwashing; the destruction of memory with chemical agents such as *puromycin,* an antibiotic that halts the synthesis of protein molecules, apparently by inhibiting the normal functioning of RNA. Both RNA and protein molecules are believed to be essential to the maintenance of memory. Animal experiments indicate that injections of puromycin can obliterate even very well-established memories.

*Microsurgery*—Techniques employing microsurgical tools to "operate" at the cellular level of development; important in cloning and other aspects of genetic engineering. Among microsurgical tools are *microsyringes* only one thousandth of a millimeter in diameter and *micropipettes,* hairlike tubes with internal diameters of fifteen thousandths of a millimeter and less.

*Molecular neurology*—A pendant of molecular biology concerned specifically with molecular events within the nervous system and particularly within the cells of the brain.

*Mongolism*—A condition of congenital idiocy; one of many genetic defects that can be detected prior to birth through karyotyping of chromosomes.

*Morning-after birth-control pill*—Acts through the mother's blood stream to destroy the embryo after it has attached itself to the lining of the uterus; demonstrated effective in animal studies but not yet approved for human use; some maintain that its use amounts to abortion.

*Mother surrogates*—Can refer either to artificial wombs or to women who may, in the near future, have implanted in their wombs the embryos of other women. Such mother surrogates might be women unable to produce eggs of their own or they might be hirelings, paid to carry embryos of other women through to term —at which point they would be required to relinquish the babies to their real, genetic mothers.

*Mutation*—A relatively permanent change in hereditary material resulting in new individuals basically unlike their parents. Mutations occur spontaneously in nature but controlled mutations are possible with genetic manipulation.

*Nidation*—Implanting of the embryo in the lining of the uterus.

*Nucleic acids*—DNA and RNA, the long-chain molecules of the cell nucleus that contain the "blueprints" for the construction of the entire organism.

*Ovum*—The female sex cell, the female egg. At birth, the female ovaries contain more than half a million egg cells, though only a few hundred of these mature during a normal lifetime. One is released each month —alternating between left and right ovary—constituting *ovulation.*

*Paleogenesis*—Life generated from two sex cells obtained

at points distant in time; paleogenetic offspring could be born to parents who have been long dead.

*Parahuman*—A hybrid consisting of human and animal material; it has been suggested that parahuman creatures might be created with genetic engineering to take care of low-grade labor; example of the misuse that genetic engineering could conceivably be put to.

*Parthenogenesis*—"Virgin birth" in which reproduction is effected without fertilization of the ovum; parthenogenesis has been induced artificially in a number of animals that do not naturally possess this capability.

*Participatory evolution*—Planned evolutionary change through genetic engineering and cybernetic manipulation.

*Photosynthesis*—Synthesis of chemical compounds with the aid of radiant energy; the process by which plants exposed to sunlight form carbohydrates in chlorophyll-containing tissues. One space scientist has proposed a *photosynthetic cyborg,* a man-machine organism capable of converting sunlight directly into energy.

*Prenatal adoption*—A term coined by Dr. Jean Rostand to describe embryo implantation in women who do not produce their own ova.

*Progesterone*—A steroid hormone important in the maintenance of the female reproductive cycle.

*Protein*—Complex combinations of amino acids that form the basic building blocks of life; the combinations are governed by DNA and RNA; there is considerable evidence that protein molecules in the brain house long-term memory.

*Psychoneurobiochemeducation*—A term created by Dr. David Krech to describe the merging of psychology, molecular neurology and education. It hints at the possibility of memory transplants, education by injection and so on.

*Psychopharmacology*—The science and production of drugs with psychic and psychological effects.

*Repressor molecules*—Theoretical molecules that could be used in genetic engineering to "erase" undesired genes or nucleotides or at least render them inoperative.

*RhoGam*—A serum that successfully combats Rh disease.

*RNA*—Ribonucleic acid. Works in conjunction with DNA

to convey instructions to the working machinery of the cell.

*Robot*—Preprogramed automatons that are not linked to humans in any way.

*Sedimentation*—A method of separating androsperm from gynosperm; semen is allowed to cool and settle for a number of hours with the result that the heavier gynosperm drop into the lower stratum while the lighter androsperm occupy the upper layer of solution. Used with considerable success in the artificial insemination of animals.

*Seminal immunity*—A rare disorder in which women's immune systems create antibodies that destroy their husband's sperm cells; causes infertility; successfully treated by abstaining from intercourse for a prescribed period of time.

*Sex cells*—Sex cells or *germinal cells* contain twenty-three chromosomes each; they are the ova, in the female, and the spermatozoa, in the male.

*Sex-chromatin*—A part of the cell nucleus which, when present and visible after staining of the cell, indicates femaleness; absence of chromatin in the fetal cells indicates that the offspring will be male; this provides an easy means of determining the sex of a child prior to birth.

*Sex-linked diseases*—Hereditary diseases such as hemophilia which are passed on to offspring of only one sex. *Sex-selection techniques* will be of particular value to women who are known carriers of any of these diseases. By avoiding conception of the vulnerable sex they can help eliminate these disorders.

*Sexual dimorphism*—The ability to change sex to accommodate changing environmental factors; a property of several lower animal forms.

*Spatial correspondence*—A property of sophisticated man-machine systems in which mechanical extensions of the man correspond spatially to his dimensions, facilitating parallel movement between man and machine.

*Sperm*—The male sex cell; resembles a tadpole. The average sperm cell is 1/8000 of an inch across, and its volume is only 1/50,000 that of the average ovum. During intercourse, the male, on average, ejaculates 400 million sperm cells into the vagina.

*Sperm banks*—Repositories of frozen semen for use in artificial insemination. Human sperm has been frozen for more than ten years and still used to successfully fertilize ova. Frozen-sperm banks are also being used to pool the semen of men whose sperm count, in any one ejaculate, is too low to effect fertilization. When sufficient sperm has been gathered, it is thawed and used to artificially inseminate the man's wife.

*Superovulation*—The release from the ovaries of more than one ovum at one time. Superovulation can be artificially induced with the administration of follicle-stimulating hormone (FSH). An unintended side effect of some fertility drugs containing FSH is *superfetation,* or multiple pregnancy. Superovulation is used in animal breeding to increase the productivity of prize cows.

*Telediagnosis*—Diagnosis of a patient from a distance employing audio-visual feedback systems; a man-machine concept designed to save doctors time and to provide quicker, more efficient medical service, particularly in emergencies; in one system already under operation, doctors examine patients over closed-circuit television systems linking hospital and an airport clinic. *Telesurgery* is contemplated for the future, using remote controlled manipulators "slaved" by electronic signal to the doctor's hands and arms.

*Telefactor*—A term coined by William E. Bradley of the Institutes of Defense Analyses to describe sophisticated teleoperators linked to man with almost every conceivable sort of feedback; for use in exploring space; a type of cyborg.

*Telegenesis*—Life generated from sex cells obtained at points distant in space; telegenic offspring are born to parents who need never meet one another.

*Teleoperator*—Defined by William R. Corliss and Edwin G. Johnsen of the Atomic Energy Commission as a "general-purpose, dexterous, cybernetic machine"; a man-machine system incorporating spatial correspondence and various types of feedback; a cyborg.

*Thermography*—A diagnostic tool used by fetologists, among others. The thermograph analyzes infrared (heat) radiation from the body with such sensitivity that it can be used to detect pregnancy extremely early in term (by picking up the tiny heat rays generated by the developing fetus), to detect the presence of multiple fetuses, to determine the effects of drugs on the fetus, etc.

*Ultrasound*—High-frequency sound used to visualize the developing fetus without radiation danger; sound waves are bounced off the fetus (pulsing right through the abdominal wall of the mother). The pattern in which the sound waves bounce back is analyzed by a computer and "read out" in the form of thousands of dots on graph paper. The dots reveal the outline of the baby's head and body, thus revealing such abnormalities as hydrocephalus ("water on the brain").

*Viral transducers*—Viruses used to introduce genetic material of a specific nature into living cells; proposed as tools of genetic engineering.

*Virus*—Quasi-living agents that consist of protein shells and contain nucleic acids; the virus has none of the cellular equipment necessary to reproduce itself but does possess the ability to "take over" cells and use their reproductive equipment to replicate the viral nucleic material.

*X chromosome*—The female-producing chromosome. The egg cell always contributes an X chromosome to the embryo.

*Y chromosome*—The male-producing chromosome. Sperm cells come in two varieties, one of which carries an X chromosome while the other variety carries the Y. When an X-carrying sperm fertilizes an X-carrying egg, the resulting embryo is destined to be female. When a Y-carrying sperm penetrates the egg, the outcome will be male.

# Index